CW00932960

MIRACLE POWER

Miracle Power

JAMIE BUCKINGHAM

KINGSWAY PUBLICATIONS
EASTBOURNE

First published in the USA by
Servant Publications, PO Box 8617, Ann Arbor, Michigan

First British edition 1991

Unless otherwise indicated, biblical quotations are from the
New International Version, © 1973, 1978, 1984 by the
International Bible Society

Front cover photo: The Image Bank

British Library Cataloguing in Publication Data

Buckingham, Jamie
Miracle Power
I. Title
248.32

ISBN 0-86065-888-0

Printed in Great Britain for
KINGSWAY PUBLICATIONS LTD
1 St Anne's Road, Eastbourne, E Sussex BN21 3UN by
Richard Clay Ltd, Bungay, Suffolk
Reproduced from the original text by arrangement with
Servant Publications

PREFACE

Miracle Power

As a boy, attending a Baptist Sunday School in a little Florida town, I often sat listening to my teacher tell of the miracles of Jesus. She had not been to seminary and didn't know she was supposed to explain them away. She simply accepted the Bible at face value. She believed Jesus walked on water, gave sight to the blind, and raised Lazarus from the dead. The only miracle she had a problem with was His first one—where He turned water into wine at the wedding feast at Cana. She chose to believe Jesus turned water into grape juice and tried, rather unconvincingly, to persuade us nine-year-old boys that this was the only textual error in the Scripture. She believed the word "wine" was added by King James' translators. People in King James' day drank a lot of wine, she said, and this was their way of justifying their sin. But everyone knew Jesus was a teetotaler, just as all good Baptists should be. We kids sat, as kids do, staring at the floor. But when she got up to use the chalkboard, we all looked at each other and giggled. We wanted to believe in a Jesus who not only gave sight to the blind, but loved to stick it to the Baptists as well.

Later, as a seminary student, I found this same mentality—rationalizing the Bible to satisfy a jaded theology—among several of my professors.

Jesus really didn't speak to the wind and the waves when they grew calm, these professors believed. Actually, the wind on the Sea of Galilee often stops blowing suddenly anyway. The real miracle lies in the fact that Jesus gives peace to the inner man.

And that story where He spit on the ground and made mud and wiped it in the eyes of a blind man, causing him to see—well, the man doubtlessly had a psychosomatic blindness. When Jesus touched him, it released inner power which broke through the self-induced blindness and caused him to see.

The professors even had an explanation for the Bible story of Jesus walking on water. Actually, they said, He was standing up in a little boat. The disciples, in a larger boat, could not see over the waves and simply thought Jesus was standing on the water.

One professor, who was also a teetotaler, had a far more "scientific" explanation for the water-to-wine incident. He told us that the big jar which Jesus told the servants to fill with water had earlier been used to store the wine. The porous clay of the jars, he said, had absorbed a great deal of wine. When the jars were refilled, this time with water, it released the wine which mingled with the water.

Each miracle that Jesus performed was explained away. The man in Gadara, for instance, who was possessed with a legion of demons, was mentally unbalanced. Back then those superstitious people actually believed in demons—little devils—which could possess people. Now, thanks to modern psychology, we realize such problems are really mental illnesses.

Yet I wondered: if belief in demons is mere superstition, and Jesus really was the Son of God (who even 2000 years ago was smarter than my professors), why did *He* call them demons?

And if Jesus was not walking on the water, but standing up in a little boat, how do you explain the fact that Simon Peter got out of the big boat and walked on the water to Jesus?

And only someone who had never tasted wine could believe that wine-flavored water would be judged by the wine steward at the wedding as "the finest wine."

No, it was taking more of a miracle for me to believe

the explanations than for me to believe the miracles. I chose to believe, as my Sunday School teacher did, that Jesus had all power and could do whatever He wanted to do—and that all the miracle stories in the Bible were true.

Why, though, had I never seen a miracle?

Well, my seminary professors had an answer for that one, too. Miracles were for that particular "dispensation," they said. Their theology was based on a highly complicated set of concepts formulated from obscure passages in Daniel and Revelation. Thus, while Jesus may have performed certain miracles, that day is now past. Today we have the Bible—and that means there is no longer any need for supernatural demonstrations. It is enough to know they once happened. Today we are to accept God by faith—not sight.

Yet, deep inside, I believe—or at least I wanted to believe—that Jesus Christ was the same today as He was yesterday. That if He had the power to heal then, He still had that power. Secretly I yearned to have it also— to be able to do what Peter and John did at the gate of the Temple and speak to a man who had been crippled from birth: "In the name of Jesus of Nazareth, rise and walk."

Wouldn't that be wonderful!

Yet Jesus and His miracles were as far removed from me as Jack and the Beanstalk. He lived in another era, it seemed, an era where geese laid golden eggs and little boys could cover a lot of ground in seven-league boots. It was wonderful, remarkable . . . but it was like all fairy tales—not for now.

Then one day it happened to me.

It was a Tuesday afternoon. Six months before, while researching my first book, I had attended a meeting of the Full Gospel Business Men's Fellowship in Washington, D.C. During the course of that three day meeting, something remarkable had happened to me. I had been filled with the Holy Spirit—an experience about which I had virtually no knowledge. I knew what it meant to be a follower of Jesus Christ. In fact, I had been a believer for a number of years. But like nearly everyone else I knew, my life was without spiritual power. I readily succumbed to temptation. I was threatened by people who believed differently—especially if they were emotional in their expression of that belief. My Christian witness was without persuasion.

All that changed, however, on a Friday night in February, 1968. I was part of the congregation of 4,000 in the grand ballroom of the Shoreham Hotel in the nation's capital. At the close of the meeting the preacher gave an invitation, asking all those who wanted to be "filled with the Holy Spirit" to come forward. I knew I needed to, but pride, doubt, and confusion kept me in my seat. Suddenly I began to cry. I wound up on my knees on the floor, weeping profusely. When I arose, some 30 minutes later, I was a changed man. I had been "baptized in the Holy Spirit" right there in my place. I returned to Florida the next day, a bit stupified—but convinced, for the first time in my life, that Jesus Christ was not only alive—He was alive in me.

My wife and I had been attending a small home prayer group at a neighbor's house, just two doors away. We began listening to tapes by Kenneth Hagin, a long-time Pentecostal teacher who told story after story of wonderful miracles taking place today. I was encouraged. But fearful.

Then came that epoch Tuesday afternoon.

My wife asked me to fix a leaky kitchen faucet. I am not much of a mechanic, a fact to which my sparse tools bore evidence. In the kitchen tool drawer I found an old screwdriver—one the children had pushed into a light socket some months before. The tip of the screwdriver was jagged with weld burns. After removing the faucet with a wrench, I went to work with that horrible screwdriver, trying to remove the corroded screw which held the rubber washer in place. Holding the fixture in my left hand and the screwdriver in my right, I pressed hard against the head of the brass screw. Suddenly the tip of the screwdiver slipped out of the screwhead and rammed, full force, into the soft place between my thumb and forefinger on my left hand. I dropped the fixture and howled with pain. Then, in a foolish reflex action, I yanked the screwdriver out of my hand. When I did a sizeable chunk of flesh came out with it—clinging to the jagged edges of the welded tool.

Blood spurted everywhere and I shouted for my wife. Running into the kitchen, she saw all the blood and began screaming. I slid to the floor, holding my right hand over the spurting wound, and gasped for her to "get me something." I assumed she knew I was talking about a washcloth or compress. Instead, she ran out the front door, apparently heading to the neighbor's house to ask for prayer.

Sitting in a growing puddle of blood, I began to feel weak.

"What would Jesus do if He were here?" I asked myself.

I knew what He would do. He would reach out, touch my wounded hand, and it would be healed.

Then I thought: If Christ is really, really in me—why don't I let Him do it through me? Still holding my right hand over the deep, open wound, I began to pray—in Jesus' name. "Praying in the Spirit," the Bible calls it.

Gradually, as I prayed, I lost track of time. The pain subsided and I was vaguely aware the bleeding had stopped. But my wound was no longer the major issue.

I was lost in the wonder of the prayer, no longer praying for healing, simply "communing" with God. The Heavenly Father was there and the Holy Spirit in me was having fellowship with Him.

I finally opened my eyes and my wife was standing next to the refrigerator, looking down at me. "No one was at home," she panted. I thought she had been gone for an hour, but in reality it had been only about three or four minutes.

Gingerly, I removed my right hand from the wound. The spot between my thumb and forefinger where the ragged screwdriver had penetrated was still covered with blood. My wife knelt beside me and handed me a damp cloth. As I wiped away the blood I was aware the wound had closed. Not only had it closed, it had healed over. There was no gaping hole, no cut, not even an indentation. All I could see was a tiny scar, like a wrinkle in my hand. My wife examined my hand, also. It was healed.

That night, when I went to bed, I kept rubbing my finger over the place where the ugly wound had been. There was no roughness, no soreness. I knew, drifting off to sleep, as I know today, that the day of miracles has not passed. Jesus is not only alive. He is alive in me.

Jamie Buckingham
Palm Bay, Florida

CONTENTS

The Miracles of Jesus

(Those marked with * used in this book)

The Miracles	Matthew	Mark	Luke	John
*Leper healed	8:1-4	1:40-12	5:12-15	
Centurion's servant cured	8:5-13		7:1-10	
Peter's Mother-in-law cured	8:14-15	1:30-31	4:38-39	
*Storm stilled	8:23-27	4:37-39	8:22-25	
*Gadarene demoniac delivered	8:28-34	5:1-17	8:26-39	
*Paralytic healed	9:1-8	2:3-12	5:18-26	
Jairus' daughter cured	9:18-19,23-26	5:22-24,36-43	8:41-42,49-56	
Woman with hemorrhage cured	9:20-22	5:25-34	8:43-48	
Two blind men see	9:27-31			
Demonized man delivered	9:32-34			
Withered hand restored	12:10-13	3:1-6	6:6-11	
*5000 fed	14:15-21	6:30-44	9:10-17	6:1-14
Christ walks on water	14:22-33	6:45-52		6:16-21
Syro-Phoenician girl cured	15:21-28	7:24-30		
4000 fed	15:32-38	8:1-9		
*Demonized boy set free	17:14-21	9:14-27	9:37-43	
Tax money in fish	17:24-27			
Two blind men healed	20:29-34	10:46-52	18:35-43	
Fig tree cursed	21:18-22	11:12-21		
Deaf man healed		7:31-35		
Blind man healed		8:22-26		
Large catch of fish			5:1-11	
Widow's son resurrected			7:11-17	
Sick woman healed			3:11-17	
Man with dropsy cured			14:1-4	
Ten lepers healed			17:11-19	
Malchus' ear restored			22:50-51	
*Water turned to wine				2:1-12
Nobleman's son cured				4:46-54
*Paralyzed man healed				5:1-15
*Blind man healed				9:1-41
*Lazarus raised from dead				11:1-45
Catch of 153 fish				21:1-6
Demonized man delivered		1:23-28	4:33-37	

INTRODUCTION

Miracles: What Are They?

Any honest study of the *supernatural*, even a simple one such as this, must begin with an understanding of the *natural*.

By *natural* I am referring to things which happen by themselves, of their own accord. Things which happen without anyone making them happen.

Natural foods are those which are not tampered with, which have no additives or preservatives.

Natural childbirth is one where the process is not assisted by surgery, mechanical devices, painkillers, or anesthesia.

"Doing what comes naturally," means to allow the process to pursue its normal course.

Natural is that which you do not have to work at, which you get if you take no measures to stop it. It is the process of "letting nature have its way."

Our word "nature" comes from the Greek word *physis*, "to grow," and the Latin word *natura*, "to be born." Natural, then, (as opposed to supernatural) is that which springs up, arrives, or goes on of its own accord. It deals with the spontaneous, the unintended, the unsolicited, that which is controlled by the laws which control nature.

The Naturalist

There are two groups of people in the world: those who hold that all events have natural origin, and those who believe many events are supernatural in origin. For a number of years, since the famous Scopes trial in Tennessee, a great debate has raged in America concerning creation. Did this world come into being as a natural course of action, or was it formed by God— a supernatural event?

The naturalist believes in a vast process in space and time which is going on of its own accord. He believes every event happens because some other event has happened. For instance, the naturalist does not see the rising of the sun each morning as a miracle. He understands that the earth rotates on an axis, an imaginary pole that stretches through the globe from south to north. This earth makes an exact turn on that axis every 24 hours. As it turns it faces the sun. Thus, the rising of the sun can be predicted because the earth turns on its axis.

On the other hand, if the earth should not turn on its axis, or if that turning should be slowed—as it was when Joshua took authority over nature and commanded "the sun to stand still"—hindering the natural process—that would be a miracle.

Likewise, the naturalist does not see healing of infection by the use of an antibiotic drug as a miracle. The human body is designed to resist infection. In fact, it has its own system of antibodies, soldiers who rush to fight the evil infection. But if the body is weakened for some reason, or the infection is too massive, it may need help. The injection of additional antibodies into the system is no more than the use of additional troops to help the battle-weary antibodies already at work in the human body.

On the other hand, what if the infection is raging, and the body is losing its battle? Let's say gangrene has set in and the flesh is dead, putrifying. There are no antibiotic drugs available, but someone prays—and suddenly the infection abates, the fever subsides, and the dead flesh comes to life. That would be a miracle.

The Supernaturalist

Pure naturalism, therefore, cannot accept the idea of a God who made nature and stands outside (or works within) to direct and change it. He believes in a nature which runs on its own. The supernaturalist, however, believes there has to be more than nature working on its own. He believes that the very framework of nature and the natural law is proof of a God who exists, who has created the framework of space and time and guides the procession of systematically connected events which fill them.

The supernaturalist sees two sets of laws—two "natures" so to speak. He sees the visible laws which govern and control visible nature. These are the laws of chemistry, physics, mathematics, geology, medicine, even the laws of human behavior. The law of gravity is one of these laws. That law says if you drop a heavier-than-air object from an airplane it will fall at a pre-determined rate of speed and splatter on the earth, depending on the density of the soil it hits and the density of the object which is falling. That law can be altered, of course. If you attach a parachute to the falling object, the cloth of the chute retards the rate of speed at which the object is falling, allowing it to settle to earth rather than splatter. If you attach a jet engine to the object which is falling, that engine may have the ability to overwhelm the law of gravity by exerting an upward thrust greater than the downward tug, allowing the object to actually fly up rather than fall down—at least as long as the fuel lasts.

Eventually, though, the law of gravity will prevail, giving rise to the saying, "That which goes up must come down."

Miracles

C.S. Lewis defines "miracle" as "an interference with nature by supernatural power." This is done as God superimposes His high, invisible law over the visible laws of nature. The supernaturalist, therefore, while not denying the laws of nature, believes also in a higher set of laws which govern the "heavenlies." These laws are invisible and are activated by various factors—none of which seem consistent with our western logic.

Prayer is one of these factors which activates miracles.

So is faith.

Sometimes miracles occur when no one asked for them or even believed they were possible. Such miracles seem to take place simply because God willed them into being. All are, however, merely the imposition of God's higher law over His lower law.

For instance, when Moses and the children of Israel came to the shore of the Red Sea, which was actually an extension of the Gulf of Suez separating Egypt from the Sinai peninsula called the Yam Suf, he was faced with an impossible situation—in the natural. Behind him was the entire army of Egypt, prepared to slaughter the Hebrew slaves. In front of him was an impassable body of water. The natural ways out of this dilemma were not sufficient. They were not armed or strong enough to fight off the Egyptians. They did not have time, materials, or the ability to build a bridge across the body of water. There were no boats available. In short, they needed a miracle.

The Bible says, "the Lord drove the sea back with a strong east wind and turned it into dry land" (Exodus 14:21). God used the natural law to perform a miracle. The wind is more powerful than the water. That is a natural law. The miracle came in the timing, and in the fact the wind blew from the east. Had it blown from any other direction it would not have worked. But the east wind caused the waters to separate. The wind then continued to blow, holding the water back until the Israelites were safely on the other side. The Egyptian army, in hot pursuit, was trapped in the sea bed. Only then did God cause the wind to stop blowing, drowning the enemy and releasing the Israelites to march on toward their promised destination.

Some naturalists, reading this passage, fail to see it as a miracle. They see it as simple coincidence. To them it does not necessarily follow that because there is a God who created nature, He sometimes interferes with those natural laws. In fact, there are many people who believe in God but reject the idea of miracles. While they may accept that He is, and even accept the idea that He has created a system of laws which are higher than the visible laws of nature, they do not believe He ever allows the invisible system to impinge on the visible system.

Their reason, they say, is reason. They are schooled in western logic and cannot give credence to a God who operates in a realm which supersedes logic—often bypassing the logical sequence of thesis, antithesis, research, and conclusion. Any God who has not read Plato and Aristotle, they argue, is not God. Such people are like my Sunday School teacher who, although she could accept a God of miracles, could never believe a good Jesus would change water to wine because her culture had schooled her that wine was evil.

A Look at Nature

To better understand the nature of God we must look at the nature of nature. Granted, there are times when nature seems "out of control." Dogs may become rabid and attack neighborhood children. Men may go insane, pick up guns and kill innocent people in shopping centers and McDonald's restaurants. Rivers may flood and swallow up homes and property. Healthy cells in the body may rebel, turn cancerous, destroy, and kill. When this happens it seems nature is rebellious. But these are exceptions to the rules God has set in motion. When we study nature, when she is "in control," that is, obeying the laws of God, we have no choice but to conclude nature was designed to submit—not to rebel.

There is no way to believe that nature produced God. Nor is there any way to believe that the two—God and nature—operate independently and are self-existent. There are those who hold to this latter view, saying it is the only way to explain the problem of evil. However, that is simply a way of saying that evil needs to be explained in a way man can comprehend. Jesus never attempted to explain evil. He simply accepted it and superimposed His higher law of miracles over it when it seemed to be changing nature from the way God intended it to be.

This leaves but one possible alternative: God created nature. Thus, nature is not resisting God as an alien, but is rebelling—as we all are—against His right to rule and reign.

How then do we answer the man who says that the miracles of Jesus (or present day miracles) are not possible because they are contrary to "the laws of nature" and God will not contradict Himself? Or course, by "laws of nature" he means the known laws, or observed laws. A miracle, however, by definition, is an exception to the laws of nature. Miracles are determined by higher laws, unseen laws, the laws of the invisible kingdom.

For instance, the Bible says Mary, a virgin, gave birth to Jesus. This is a scientific impossibility. We know it, and so did Joseph, her husband. A virgin birth is contrary to the course of nature. The regular process of nature calls for a male sperm to impregnate a female egg through the act of sexual intercourse. But Mary had not "known a man." The Bible says the male sperm, which was placed in her womb by the Holy Spirit, came from God.

Impossible! Yes, unless the regular process of nature was overruled or supplemented by something from beyond nature. That is a miracle.

Miracles in the Bible—and miracles today—are always

accompanied by fear and wonder. Why? Because they are exceptions to the known. They come from the unknown. They are more than natural. They are supernatural. How can they be surprising unless they are seen as exceptions to the rules?

If you approach this subject by ruling out the supernatural you will see no miracles. You will be forced to say all such occurrences have natural causes, or are caused by natural laws yet unknown to man—in short, hang on long enough and we'll figure it out.

On the other hand, until you believe nature works according to regular laws—and regular laws alone—you will see no miracles. Until you realize the earth always follows a natural law, turning on its axis once every 24 hours, you'll not understand that what happened in the valley of Ajalon, when Joshua commanded the "sun to stand still," was a miracle. This means, contrary to what some believe, that advancing scientific knowledge does not make it harder to accept miracles, it makes it easier. The more we learn about the laws of nature the more astounding it is when God overrides those laws by superimposing His higher laws.

The Higher Law

There are those who say only an incompetent workman would create something which needs to be interfered with by the creator. But that statement assumes that God is like a general contractor who, once having built a house, leaves it and goes on to the next building project—with no interest in the house's inhabitants. The God revealed in Jesus, however, is more than a Creator—He is a Father. He has not simply created this earth long, long ago and now sits back watching. He is still creating—just as much today as when He put it all together out of nothing. Every time a male sperm touches a female egg, a new world is created. Every time a human being recognizes his need to depend on God, and calls out for Jesus Christ to save him, a new world is created. Every kind act, done in the name of Jesus, brings a new creation into being. Every song, every painting, every act of love, every literary composition—all are acts of creation as surely as the creation of an elephant or a man.

God's higher law is the law of love. Only love makes the difference. Thus, every miracle is a new creation—an act of godly love. Nature is without emotion or morality. A poisonous snake is designed to protect itself by striking. It strikes at a human being just as quickly as it strikes at a predator. It has no morals. No emotions. A miracle, such as the one recorded in Acts 28:1-6, is an act of morality, an act of love, an act of new creation. In that remarkable story, told by Luke—a physician, by the way—we find the story of Paul, shipwrecked on the island of Malta, bitten by a poisonous viper. The islanders, knowing how deadly the snake was, expected him "to swell up or suddenly fall over dead." But nothing happened to him. As a result, the people were able to hear him when he told them about God. Not only that, but Paul visited a number of sick people on the island—including the chief official— laid hands on them, and they were healed. God's higher law of love had overriden the natural law which says poison in a man's system brings death.

God's higher law is based on love. "God so loved the world," Jesus told Nicodemus, "that He gave His one and only Son, that whoever believes in Him shall not perish but have eternal life" (John 3:16). That is the law of love.

The reason we have a tough time believing in miracles is we believe all things were made for man. Not so. God loves man and for man's sake became a man and died for him. But all things were not made for man—they were made for God. "The earth is the Lord's," David said correctly. Isaiah reminds us the earth is God's footstool. Man lives here as a tenant farmer might occupy the land of a wealthy land baron—with God's permission and for God's pleasure.

The skeptic asks how we can then believe that such a mighty God would ever condescend to "come down" to this tiny planet. That question, however, would sound utterly ridiculous if we knew all there is to know about God's creation. Perhaps one of these days we'll discover there are rational creatures on some of those other bodies that float in space. When we find them we may also discover that they, like us, have fallen and need redemption. But what if we discover that unlike us, their Adam and Eve did not sin? That their planet remains an Edenic paradise where God rules and reigns, and all nature responds to the laws of God?

It is possible, you know, that this universe may be filled with happy lives which have never needed to be redeemed by blood sacrifice. Or, it may be their redemption came in modes different from the one God ordained for Planet Earth. Maybe the Son of God came to their planet not as a Jewish Jesus, but as a four-legged beaktheon.

He who questions how a big God could come down to little earth knows only a little God—the size of man. The bigger our concept of God, the more we see Him as a God of miracles.

Miracles reveal the nature of God. Thus, there are no big miracles and little miracles. All miracles are big—for they reflect the nature of our big God. While they do, by definition, interrupt the usual course of nature, in so doing they assert all the more the unity and harmony of God. They reveal a God who not only created nature, but who still controls it by the higher law of love. "The creation waits in eager expectation," Paul wrote, "for the sons of God to be revealed" (Romans 8:19). In short, all nature yearns for man to take his rightful place as a being of spiritual authority through whom miracles come as readily as they did though Jesus—the second Adam.

This world is interested in miracles. You can go into any bar in America, any pub in Europe, strike up a conversation about miracles, and you'll get a crowd—especially if you're talking about one that happened to you. Folks will gather around. You don't have to be in church—in fact, usually there is more interest in bars than in churches, perhaps because miracles are so rare in today's church. As a result, church people have made up all kinds of explanations for why they don't happen anymore.

But miracles were at the very heart of Jesus' ministry, for He came to reveal God—and God is a God of miracles.

Unlike Jesus, John the Baptist did not seem to be a miracle-worker. With the exception of Elijah and Elisha, most of the prophets did not have a miracle ministry. Jesus, however, was a minister of miracles. Every place He went, miraculous things happened. His followers, into whom He had breathed His Spirit, were also ministers of miracles. The instruction the Holy Spirit gave to the early church was that the church was to be a church of miracles, a church of the supernatural.

Miracles should be the norm in the life of the Christian. Because we are constantly stumbling through a dark world, we need God to guide our footsteps, giving us the ability to walk supernaturally.

That means miracles. But God is not restoring miracles to the church. They've been there all along. He is simply waiting for simple people who will step forward in faith and expect God to use them, as He used Jesus, to perform miracles.

As I said earlier, that's a bit frightening. It's frightening because it demands we become partakers of the supernatural world in which God lives. It's frightening because it calls for us to be willing to become instruments of God's Spirit. It is at this very point that so many draw back. It is one thing to worship an impersonal God who never threatens us with His presence any more than a book on the shelf threatens us. But it is always shocking to meet Life when we thought we were alone. "Look out!" we cry. "Something's out there!" Indeed it is. Not something—but Someone. And sensing He is so much bigger than we are, we find it easier to cut the line than to reel it in and run the risk of having it consume us.

Someplace I heard the story of the little boy whose mother put him to bed in the upstairs bedroom. After kissing him goodnight, she went back downstairs to read the paper. Moments later the little boy, dressed in his pajamas, was half-way down the stairs himself.

"Mommy, I'm afraid."

"There's nothing to be afraid of, I was just up there."

"But it's dark in my room."

"Don't be afraid; God is in there. Now go back to bed."

The little fellow crept back up the steps and stood at the door of his dark bedroom, peering in. "God," he said in a shaky voice. "I'm coming in, but don't You move 'cause if You do You'll scare me to death."

Today we discover God is moving—and a lot of folks are scared. He is alive, pulling at our line, perhaps approaching at the speed of light. And now, those of us who have been dabbling in religion are suddenly forced to make a decision. Do we go on, or do we turn and flee?

If we do go on, if we reel in the line, if we enter the dark room, we need to know there are no limits to what God may choose to do to—and through—us. I challenge you to study these miracles of Jesus not as ancient history, but as a prelude to what He wants to do through you.

Today. These accounts are either lies of the first magnitude, or history. If they are lies, then the entire Bible is false and Jesus is the biggest con man who ever walked the face of the earth. But if they are history, then we have no choice but to allow the same Spirit which raised Christ from the dead to come into us. Once that happens we, too, will become ministers of miracles.

A modern day prophet stopped by my house during the days I was writing this introduction to *Miracle Power* and left a "prophecy" he said he had received from God. I put it aside for a number of days, busy with other things. Then, shortly before I finished this little book, I took it down and read it. I include it here as confirmation of what I have just written:

"The health of My people is not dependent upon what they do, but rather what I choose to let happen. I do not will that any of My people be sick, but rather that they have life and health in abundance. There are laws and practices that I have set into motion with regard to the health of My people; and when those laws and practices are violated, those who have violated them will receive the 'just reward' of that violation. The miracle of healing takes place when I choose to intervene in the process that follows, by diverting or absorbing that motion and thus nullifying its effect. But what will cause Me to intervene in any given situation is not a matter of faith, supplications, or even prayer. I am sovereign, and make all decisions based on My sovereignty. I alone am the healer and giver of life. My Word says that faith is important to the healing process. That is true. But it is not, in and of itself, the magical or mystical key to unlock the storehouse of health and well-being, but rather a necessary part of the process of healing. The presence of faith is a catalyst to begin the process, but if all the elements are not there, there is no change—no miracle.

"I shall never allow man to fully understand the healing process, for if he does, he will give himself credit and lessen his dependence upon Me. There will continue to be those times when I choose to allow sickness and disease to bend and to break the rebellious spirit. That, too, is for Me to decide. No man shall ever fully understand My process.

"Knowing this does not release you from living a holy life of faith, or of doing those things you know to be good which produce health. Only the fool will omit that which he knows is right. Rather, you should continue to exercise your faith and believe in Me, and who I am, and in who you are in Me. I have allowed some to have limited access to understanding this mystery. Some physicians have tapped, superficially, into that vein. Many have been healed by doctors who have limited knowledge of the mystery. Others have been healed by the touch of some of My chosen ones. But that is still My choice, for man can go only as far as I am willing to let him in this process of understanding. I will never reveal the full truth and understanding, for that would make man like Me and he would depart even farther from full truth.

"Do not allow this lack of understanding to dismay you; rather, let it draw you closer to Me. In doing this you will experience more health and release than you could ever imagine possible."

The purpose of this book is to stimulate you, excite you, hopefully to convince you that the miracles of Jesus were not for yesterday—they are for today. They were not for Jesus alone; they are for you. It is not enough to say, "Expect a miracle." We should say, "Expect a miracle through me."

ONE

NOTHING BUT THE BEST
Jesus Turns Water into Wine

"Miracles reveal the nature of God. Not only is God a joyful God, He wants us filled with joy, too..."

JOHN 2:1-11

On the third day a wedding took place at Cana in Galilee. Jesus' mother was there, and Jesus and His disciples had also been invited to the wedding. When the wine was gone, Jesus' mother said to Him, "They have no more wine."

"Dear woman, why do you involve Me?" Jesus replied. "My time has not yet come."

His mother said to the servants, "Do whatever He tells you."

Nearby stood six stone water jars, the kind used by the Jews for ceremonial washing, each holding from twenty to thirty gallons. Jesus said to the servants, "Fill the jars with water"; so they filled them to the brim.

Then He told them, "Now draw some out and take it to the master of the banquet."

They did so, and the master of the banquet tasted the water that had been turned into wine. He did not realize where it had come from, though the servants who had drawn the water knew. Then he called the bridegroom aside and said, "Everyone brings out the choice wine first and then the cheaper wine after the

guests have had too much to drink; but you have
saved the best till now."

This, the first of His miraculous signs, Jesus performed
in Cana of Galilee. He thus revealed His glory, and His
disciples put their faith in Him.

If you were the Son of God, and you had only three
years to convince the world that God is a God of love
and miracles, where would you perform your first miracle?

On the portico of the great Temple in Jerusalem?

Perhaps during an intermission at one of the festivals
in the stadium?

Maybe you'd call a press conference at the Herodian
Court?

Not Jesus. He chose the most common and natural place
imaginable—the wedding reception at the home of a
friend.

The miracles of Jesus fall into five general categories:
(1) *Miracles of healing*. These include giving sight to the
blind, healing cripples, and curing diseases such as leprosy.
(2) *Miracles over nature*. These miracles include such
instances as walking on water and stilling the Galilean
storm. (3) *Miracles of deliverance*. Stories abound of Jesus
setting people free from evil spirits. Some of these people
had been made sick by the demons, but when Jesus
commanded the demons to leave they were healed as well.
(4) *Miracles of resurrection*. On several occasions Jesus spoke
life back into dead bodies. Indeed, He experienced such
a miracle Himself near the close of His earthly ministry.
(5) *Miracles of creation*. In these miracles Jesus brought
things into being which had not been there before. On
one occasion food was provided for 5,000 people on a
hillside. On another occasion water was turned into wine.

It was this miracle, a miracle of creation, that Jesus
performed to begin His public ministry—just as the first

recorded act of His Father was the creation of the entire earth.

The purpose for all miracles is to glorify God. Miracles have no other purpose. All miracles come from God and are designed so God gets the glory and the credit. God does not want man to get the credit or the glory. He is displeased when men or women allow themselves to be called miracle-workers. He doesn't want churches to brag that they are miracle-working churches. When that sort of thing happens, God takes the power away and gives it to those who give Him all the glory. God will not share His glory with any other.

Jesus knew that, which is probably one of the reasons He began His public miracle ministry in such an unobtrusive manner. It took place at Cana, a small, terraced community on a steep mountainside near Jesus' hometown of Nazareth—just a few miles west and south of the Sea of Galilee. Cana of Galilee is not to be confused with the other Cana in Coelo-Syria. This was a tiny village less than a mile from Nazareth.

Cana was located in the region where the ancient tribe of Asher had settled. Many years before, when old Jacob lay dying, he had prophesied about each of his sons. His prophecy for Asher seemed strange: "Asher's food will be rich; he will provide delicacies fit for a king" (Genesis 49:20). Now, at a wedding feast in Cana, that prophecy was about to come to pass.

The people of Israel, especially in the northern regions around the Sea of Galilee, were close-knit. Everyone knew everyone else. A stranger in the village would have been spotted immediately. Jesus had grown up here. His mother and father, Mary and Joseph, were well known. They, too, had grown up here. Jesus had attended the synagogue schools, played with the neighborhood children, and for a number of years had worked with His father in the family carpenter shop.

While the people of Nazareth and Cana respected Jesus as a hard-working young bachelor, they had no concept of His real identity. However, about a month before this wedding took place, Jesus had taken off His carpenter's apron and headed south along the rich Jordan Valley toward Jericho. Something was changing in His life. He had now passed His 30th birthday—the minimum age at which a man could be known as a *rabbi*, or teacher. Jesus may not have been aware of all that was happening in His life, but even then He was following the inner voice, listening to God. At this point it may have been more instinct than obedience. As a bird knows when it is time to fly south, and a chipmunk knows when to store nuts for the winter ahead, Jesus knew it was time to turn His back on the carpenter's shop and head south. He must have said to His mother, "It is time. I must lay aside my carpentering and venture out to that which my real Father now calls Me." Jesus had been tutored well by His step-father, Joseph. But now Joseph was dead. Jesus could leave the family business in the hands of His younger brothers. It was time to fulfill His destiny. Only Mary would have understood.

Some place between that spot where the peaceful Jordan flows out of the southern tip of the Sea of Galilee and the ancient city of Jericho near the Dead Sea, Jesus stopped beside the narrow Jordan River. He had heard reports that His cousin, John the Baptist, a prophet, had finally left the Judean wilderness where he had lived for years and was calling the people to repent of their sins against God. As an indication of their repentance, they were asking John to immerse them in the Jordan River in the ritual of water baptism. That morning, standing on the west bank of the Jordan, Jesus listened as John—whom He had not seen in years—preached. His message had not varied from the day he began preaching: "I baptize you with water for repentance. But after me will come one who is more powerful than I, whose sandals I am not fit to carry. He will baptize you with the Holy Spirit and with fire. . . ."

Suddenly John's eyes locked in on the figure of Jesus, standing by Himself apart from the crowd. Whether John instantly recognized Him as the son of his mother's cousin we do not know. What we do know was that John's mother, Elizabeth, was "filled with the Holy Spirit," and had imparted that Spirit to her son. Now that Spirit in John recognized His eternal counterpart, the Son of God, the Second Person of the Trinity, standing on the river bank. Although it was John who cried out, it was the Holy Spirit who gave the joyful utterance: "Look, the lamb of God who takes away the sin of the world."

Rushing through the water to Jesus, John pled, "I need to be baptized by You." Jesus refused, saying He had come for John to immerse Him in water. When that happened, a dove descended and the people heard a voice: "This is My Son, Whom I love, with Him I am well pleased."

The next day a man called Andrew, who had been at the baptism service, brought his brother Simon (later called Peter) to Jesus saying, "We have found the Messiah."

Thus, even though the people of Nazareth and Cana did not recognize Jesus as anyone other than the son of Mary and Joseph, others from outside the region were beginning to realize Jesus was the Messiah—the Son of God.

Following this, Jesus climbed the high desert mountains to the west of the Jordan into one of the most forsaken regions on earth—the Judean wilderness. He remained there for a period of 40 days, fasting and praying. At the end of this time He was tempted by Satan who tried to get Him, among other things, to turn rocks into bread and feed the hungry. Jesus resisted the temptations and the Bible says He returned to Galilee "in the power of the Spirit."

It was this power—which had come upon Him when He received the Holy Spirit during His baptism—that enabled Him to perform miracles. The only question was: where would He perform His first miracle?

> *On the third day a wedding took place at Cana in Galilee. Jesus' mother was there, and Jesus and His disciples had also been invited to the wedding.*

So we come to a normal social occasion, a festive wedding to be held in a home in Cana. Mary, Jesus' mother, was there. In fact, she seems to have had a special place at the wedding. There is no mention of Joseph. Perhaps he had already died, for Mary is the center of attention in the story. One of the Coptic gospels—an Egyptian biography of Jesus which was not included in the original canon of the Scripture—states that Mary was a sister of the bridegroom's mother. And one of the early prefaces to the books of the New Testament, the Monarchian Prefaces, says the bridegroom was John, the son of Salome, who was the sister of Mary. Thus, if it was, indeed, Mary's nephew who was getting married, it would explain why Aunt Mary had such a prominent place at the festival. There is a lot of legend mixed in these ancient stories, but this much is true—Mary occupied a primary role at the wedding feast.

It was a typical village wedding feast. Jewish law called for the wedding of a virgin to begin on Wednesday. But like all weddings, this one lasted more than one day. The wedding ceremony itself took place late in the evening after a feast. After dinner the young couple would be escorted through the village streets to their new home with the light of flaming torches and a canopy over their heads. For a week they maintained an open house and were treated like kings and queens. In a land where there was much poverty, where men had to toil in the earth, pull fishing nets, or herd animals for a living, where women did hard physical labor and all were looked upon as chattels by the oppressive Roman government, this week of wedding festivities was a supreme occasion in life.

The highlight of the Jewish wedding then, as it is today, is the reciting of the *bracha*, the Jewish blessings. This custom, like the *huppa* canopy, the ring, the *ketuba* (marriage contract), and the breaking of the wine glass, has great meaning to those of the Jewish faith. The *bracha* is actually "seven benedictions" *(va brachot)* which are recited at the wedding ceremony and during the seven days following it. Although usually recited by the rabbi, they are not blessings which the rabbi bestows on the married couple. Rather, they are statements about the meaning of marriage which the couple proclaim. They are recited by the rabbi to spare illiterate brides and grooms public embarrassment. After they are recited, the bride and groom are entitled to drink the ceremonial wine over which the blessing was made.

The seven blessings start with the blessing over the cup of wine. The wine has no ceremonial significance but is drunk, as on Sabbaths and at festivals, to set the mood of joy which the occasion calls for.

Bracha number two acknowledges creation. "Blessed are you, O Lord, our God, King of the universe, who has created everything to His glory." The world is not a meaningless accident. Marriage is a re-enactment of the act of divine creation. The couple, by bonding together, continue life in this world for the glory of God.

The third bracha acknowledges that we were created by God as humans, with all the privileges and obligations that come with it.

The fourth blessing states we are endowed with the divine image. The ability to express this sexually, and so create new life, completes the purpose for which we are here—to create and re-create as God does.

The fifth bracha is a reminder that a home is never personal—it is public. As the exiles should return to Jerusalem, so the home should be a place where exiles are always welcome.

The sixth blessing reminds the couple and their friends that weddings should be a time of rejoicing.

The final bracha, which concludes the wedding ceremony, acknowledges that we are capable of genuine rejoicing, real friendship, deep love. It is at this point the wine is served—first to the couple, then to all the guests.

> *When the wine was gone, Jesus' mother said to Him, "They have no more wine."*
>
> *"Dear woman, why do you involve me?" Jesus replied, "My time has not yet come." His mother said to the servants, "Do whatever He tells you."*

During this happy time Jesus and His disciples attended the festivities. Jesus had just met these "disciples" three days before. At that time He had called only five men to follow Him. They were strangers to the people in town, but because of the respect they had for Jesus, they welcomed His friends also. Thus, while Jesus was invited, the disciples just showed up—which may be one of the reasons the wine ran out. Any modern hostess understands this problem. She plans, as Mary did, for a certain number of people. Then the son shows up at the reception with ten thirsty friends, and everything goes out of control. The wine ran out. No wonder Mary came to Jesus and said, "What are You going to do about this?"

For a Jewish feast wine was essential. "Without wine,"

the ancient rabbis said, "there is no joy." As usual, fresh
wine was served at the weddings—not the kind that had
been kept around and aged for a long time.

Drunkenness, however, was forbidden. The Scriptures
commanded against it.

> Who has woe? Who has sorrow?
> Who has strife? Who has complaints?
> Who has needless bruises? Who has bloodshot eyes?
>
> Those who linger over wine, who go to sample
> bowls of mixed wine. Do not gaze at wine when it
> is red, when it sparkles in the cup, when it goes down
> smoothly!
>
> In the end it bites like a snake and poisons like
> a viper.   (Proverbs 23:29-32)

In times past, when God's chosen people had disobeyed
in this matter, He had removed His blessing from the
entire nation. Thus, while the people loved to drink wine,
they were careful not to get drunk, for they feared the
wrath of God. To keep this from happening, it was a
common practice to mix the wine with water—two parts
of wine to three parts of water.

This was a common practice not only at weddings, but
at the Passover as well, where the Gemara—one of the
Jewish documentary guides—commanded: "The cup of
blessing is not to be blessed until it is mixed with water."

Wine is the only alcoholic drink mentioned in the Bible.
(The process of distilling beverages to produce "hard
liquor" was unknown until the 13th century.) Wine was
the common drink of the New Testament. There were
four basic kinds of wine:

Oxos (Matthew 27:48, Mark 15:36) was a type of vinegar.
It was the kind of wine offered to Jesus when He hung

on the cross.

Gleuchos, a sweet wine, was also known as "new wine." It was a stronger drink, the kind the disciples were accused of drinking in Acts 2 when they were filled with the Holy Spirit and spoke in tongues.

Sikera (Luke 1:15) was a grain wine, although sometimes made from dates or honey. It was highly intoxicating.

Oinos (Revelation 14:10) was pure wine, made from grapes. It was sometimes referred to as *genema tes ampelou,* or fruit of the vine (Luke 22:18). Although fermented, it was not always inebriating, being only slightly alcoholic like the *vin ordinaire* of France or perhaps like today's wine cooler, which is a mixture of low alcohol wine and fruit juice. While Paul tells young Timothy his church leaders should never drink to excess, he advises Timothy to stop drinking water and use a little wine *(oinos)* to ease his stomach pains. It is significant to note that the wine Jesus created at the wedding feast in Cana was *oinos*— and like all wines at weddings, it was mixed with water.

What do you do if you are the hostess at a wedding reception with your son, who has recently been publicly recognized as the Son of God, as a guest, and the wine runs out? A shortage of wine at your wedding might not be a big deal when compared to world hunger, the oppression of the Roman Empire, or even the huge number of people who have leprosy. But it was a big deal to Mary, because she was responsible. She was the official hostess. If the wine ran out, she was at fault. While other things might bring pain to others, this brought pain to her. What did she do? She could have gone to the bridegroom and told him to send out for more wine. But instead, she went straight to the fountainhead. She approached her oldest son, Jesus, and told Him of the problem.

His reply seems almost discourteous: "Why are you telling me? My time has not yet come." A better understanding of what He said would be, "Don't worry. Leave things to Me. Let Me handle it My own way."

And He did.

At this point we need to understand who Jesus was. He was the Son of God, God manifest on earth. The reason He came was so people could see what God is like. He came to show us that God is a miracle-working God. While God has set in motion all the laws of the universe, He remains in charge of everything. He's the boss. He's the "Man." This is His universe. This is His world. He created it. It runs by His natural laws, but He can, at any time He wants, override those laws with the higher laws of love and miracles. Jesus came as a miracle-working individual to reveal that His Father is a miracle-working God.

His mother, Mary, knew that. She had known it from the time the angel came to her as a virgin and told her she would conceive a baby, not from man's sperm, but by a miraculous touch of God. After the baby was born in Bethlehem she had been visited by shepherds and wise men alike, all saying God had spoken to them about this marvelous child—the Son of God. For thirty years she had "pondered these things in her heart." Now her son had entered His public ministry. It was time for things to happen.

Turning to the servants she said, "Do whatever He tells you."

What did she think He was going to say? "Go down to the convenience store and pick up a couple of bottles of Mogen David"? She knew better than that. She knew something marvelous was about to happen. There was a growing excitement at this moment. While the celebration was going on—the dancing, the laughing, the congratulating—the real excitement was what was about to happen.

> *Nearby stood six water jars, the kind used for ceremonial washing, each holding from twenty to thirty gallons. Jesus said to the servants. "Fill the jars with water"; so they filled them to the brim. Then He told them, "Now draw some out and take it to the master of the banquet."*

The Jews were notorious for ceremonial washing. Mark, in talking about the Jews, said: "The Pharisees and all the Jews do not eat unless they give their hands a ceremonial washing...." (Mark 7:3). A crowd of any size meant there had to be water present, lots of it, to accommodate the washing the Jews went through.

Nearby stood six stone water jars, the kind used by the Jews for ceremonies of hand and foot washing, each holding 20 to 30 gallons. Perhaps you have seen these big jars or pictures of them. They stood outside the doors and were used for ceremonial cleansing. At orthodox Jewish weddings, the water from the jars was used for the washing of hands because you could not enter an orthodox house during the ceremony without ceremonial cleansing. Cups, dishes, even pots and pans went through a ceremonial washing before each use. The wedding feast was a dinner of many courses. Between each course the servants would come with water and basin. Each guest would join in the ritual as the water was poured over his hands in ceremonial washing. Even today, if you visit an orthodox Jewish restaurant in Israel you will find water to be used for the washing of hands prior to the meal. In Jesus' day, anybody who entered the house for the wedding not only washed his hands, but had his feet washed by servants. The land was arid, dusty. Most people wore sandals. A few went barefooted. Everyone had dirty feet. Servants were provided to wash them during festive occasions. Three years later, the night before He was crucified, Jesus once again referred to the ceremony of washing feet. In a beautiful, personal demonstration, He picked up the basin and towel and washed His disciples' feet, saying God's people should be servants and should wash each other's feet.

At the wedding all this water was necessary—180 gallons of it—for ceremonial cleansing. The six urns, now only partially filled to their full 30 gallon capacity, sat outside the door. Jesus told the servants to fill them up, drawing water from a nearby well or cistern. Then He said, "Now draw some out and take it to the master of the banquet."

The master of the banquet was the maitre d', the head waiter, the head servant. The servants poured the water into a smaller container and took it to the master of the banquet. He, in turn, tasted it, discovered it was excellent wine, and called for the bridegroom.

I cannot help but stand amazed at Jesus' confidence and authority. He did not say, "Let Me taste it first." He told the servants to take it to the head waiter and let him taste it. Even though it was His first miracle, He was operating with the greatest assurance imaginable. He knew what had happened. There was no need for Him to test it out. Now it was just a matter of letting the others in on the miracle.

Question: Where did the miracle take place? Did it take place in the urn? That meant they now had 180 gallons of wine. Did it take place as it was dipped out of the urn into the smaller container? Did it take place as it was poured into the cup? Or did it take place as the maitre d' tasted it? Was it water up until the time he tasted it?

The Scriptures are silent as to exactly when and how the miracle took place. But that's because miracles, by their very nature, are unexplainable.

The important thing is not where or when it took place, but the transformation.

The master of the banquet tasted the water that had been turned into wine, not realizing where it had come from. He called the bridegroom aside and said, "Everyone brings out the choice wine first and then the cheaper wine. But you have saved the best till now."

That which was transformed was better than that which was manufactured. This is one of the vast incomprehensibles about God. The things of God are always better than the things of man. Everything we make with our hands is secondary to that which God makes and transforms.

It is meaningful that Jesus chose an ordinary ceremony—a wedding—to perform His first miracle. God always uses the ordinary. When the angel came to Mary to tell her she had conceived, he met her—not in the Temple—but in a private place. When it was time for the Son of God to be born, He was birthed in a stable. It was shepherds who received the first angelic visit. The Son of God spent His early years in a carpenter's shop. God is a God of the ordinary. How appropriate that the first miracle would be at the wedding of a nameless village peasant who was suffering the embarrassment of having run out of wine. Jesus wanted us to know that not only does God enjoy celebrations—He is a God of the ordinary. Miracles are not reserved for heads of state, missionaries and television preachers—they are for us. They take place in impossible situations—when the wine runs out—to teach us man's extremity is God's opportunity, and that delays of mercy are not to be construed as the denials of prayer.

Jesus never put restrictions on miracles. He never conditioned a miracle by saying, "If you will become a Christian then God will give you a miracle." Miracles, He indicates, are for everyone—believer and non-believer alike. The wine was for all. But there were those at the wedding who were "called." They had chosen to follow Jesus. They were the greatest beneficiaries. Most just enjoyed the wine and went on about their merriment. But those who knew it was Jesus who had changed the water into wine did more—they became believers in a miracle-working God. Years later, they, too, enjoyed the same power that Jesus had.

The marvelous part of God's grace is how He pours it out on everybody. The rain falls on the just and the unjust. It doesn't just fall on the crops of the Christians. It falls on both sides of the road. When God pours out His grace, He pours it out on all of us.

Most of us have never seen water turned to wine. But a number of people have experienced God's miraculous provision. On several occasions, a poor woman in our church in Florida discovered the food in her refrigerator was being restored, day after day. She would go to bed at night with only a few swallows of milk left in the milk carton—not enough to give to her child the next day. Awaking in the morning, she would find the carton almost filled.

More important, she testified, was the new joy God put in her heart day after day—the kind of joy a bride feels at a wedding.

The evidences remain. Whenever Jesus comes into a life, there is a new quality. What He does is sparkling. His new wine is never flat. It bubbles. It's spumonte. Exciting. Exhilarating. Thrilling. The life that Jesus brings is rich and full—nothing but the best as He takes the water of our lives and turns it into wine.

Lord, I want to be like Jesus, one who brings the sparkle and excitement of the Holy Spirit to those who think life is flat and tasteless. I ask for that power—and the wisdom to use it for Your glory.

Two

Power Over Nature
Jesus Calms the Storm

"Who is this? Even the wind and the waves obey Him!"

MARK 4:35-41
(also Matthew 8:23-27 and Luke 8:22-25)

That day when evening came, He said to His disciples, "Let us go over to the other side." Leaving the crowd behind, they took Him along, just as He was, in the boat. There were also other boats with Him. A furious squall came up, and the waves broke over the boat, so that it was nearly swamped. Jesus was in the stern, sleeping on a cushion. The disciples woke Him and said to Him, "Teacher, don't you care if we drown?"

He got up, rebuked the wind and said to the waves, "Quiet! Be still!" Then the wind died down and it was completely calm.

He said to His disciples, "Why are you so afraid? Do you still have no faith?"

They were terrified and asked each other, "Who is this? Even the wind and the waves obey Him!"

For years, as a boy, I read and heard the miracle stories of Jesus. However, I never could translate them over into my world for today. I heard about them in Sunday School. Occasionally, the preacher would mention one of them in his sermons. But they never seemed real. I knew I had to deal with them because they were in the Bible. But since neither I nor anyone else I knew had ever seen a miracle—or if we had seen one we were afraid to call it a miracle—we didn't have anything to relate it to. That meant we had to come up with some really cockeyed theories to try to explain why miracles don't occur today. Most of the Christians I was around, in fact, went to great lengths to figure out what must have really happened in those old Bible stories.

Later, in college, and finally in seminary where I studied theology, my professors studiously and ceremoniously attempted to explain away the miracles.

Yet, in my heart I knew there had to be another kingdom out there—an invisible kingdom—that Jesus lived in and drew His power from in order to work miracles in this visible world in which we live.

So, in this world of reason and logic, I struggled with the possibility (yea, the probability) of another dimension—the dimension of the spiritual world. Deep in my heart I always believed the miracles were real and were for today. At times I would daydream, thinking how wonderful it would be for me to lay hands on a sick person and see him healed.

I remember the day, when I was about six years old, that we had a big forest fire which burned right up to the front yard of our rural home in Florida. My father and some of his hired hands who worked in the citrus groves were desperately fighting to keep it away from our new house, located right at the edge of the woods. The lone firetruck from the little town, about two miles away, was there. All the two firemen could do was spray water on the roof of our house, trying to keep it from igniting. The fire raged on, a hot wind blowing the flames until they licked the side of the house, causing the paint to blister, then begin to smolder.

My mother, nearly hysterical, told us little kids to go inside and pray—only a "miracle" could save our house from the flames. I ran inside and knelt down beside a big chair. In simple faith I asked God to turn the fire around and put out the flames. When I went back outside the wind had changed. The fire was blowing back on itself. Within moments it quickly died out.

That night, at dinner, my father told us how lucky we were that the wind had changed its course. I kept waiting for him to tell us God had done it, but he attributed it all to "good fortune." I was crushed, for I wanted so desperately to believe God had answered my prayers and sent a miracle.

Even when I didn't understand who Jesus was, I really did believe there was a God who did supernatural things. If He was God, then He must be big enough to heal people, put out forest fires, and calm the seas. I wanted to believe, but whenever I saw a miracle, people around me tried to convince me it wasn't God who did it.

Today I have reached a place in my own personal pilgrimage where I believe miracles are not only for today— they are for me and for the church.

Nothing frustrates people more than our inability to take authority over inanimate objects. People take great satisfaction in training animals, in discovering new ways to combat disease, in solving mathematical and scientific problems. We feel fulfilled when faced with a problem—such as trying to figure out how to build a bridge across a river—and in solving that problem using engineering, construction, economic and managerial skills. We have developed vaccines which have virtually wiped out diseases such as polio, smallpox, and bubonic plague. We have learned that it is possible to set and splint broken bones, meaning people don't have to have their bodies disfigured for life simply because they broke a leg as a child.

But there are certain things man hasn't been able to do

anything about. The weather is one of them. We can barely predict it. We have weather forecasters and meteorologists and hurricane specialists. We send up weather balloons, fly airplanes into the center of hurricanes, and forecast weather patterns from satellites. But forecasting and reporting is all we can do. No one has yet figured out how to change, much less control, the weather. As a result, even the finest humanitarian events, such as a presidential inauguration, can be wiped out by a blizzard; the finest church events, such as an evangelistic meeting in a stadium, can be devastated by a rain shower. In short, we simply can't do anything about the weather.

In early 1987 the National Aeronautics and Space Administration launched a $55 million satellite called GOES-H (Goestationary Operational Environmental Satellite). It was pushed into space by a Delta rocket costing $40 million. The satellite, which now orbits the equator 25,876 miles above the earth at its apogee (high point), is the most sophisticated weather satellite in the world. But all it can do is relay signals from 10,000 automated ground stations to report on the location of clouds, rainfall, river levels, snow depths and temperatures. It can report on the weather but it cannot control it.

We mere mortals can do even less. When the satellite reports that a hurricane is coming, all we can do is get ready. In Florida, where I live, that means we batten down, store water, get out the kerosene lanterns, make sure we have batteries for the radio, and, if we live in low areas in the path of the storm, flee for our lives. Even the U.S. Navy, the most powerful sea force in the world, is helpless. It sends its big ships out to sea to ride out the storm rather than leaving them in a harbor where they may be battered against the shore. It's just as Jesus said—the "wind blows wherever it pleases" (John 3:8). We can't do anything about it.

Several years ago Pat Robertson, then president of the

Christian Broadcasting Network in Virginia Beach, Virginia, was featured in the news when he called his viewers into prayer and rebuked a hurricane. The hurricane responded, changing its trajectory. Instead of hitting the Tidewater area as predicted, it veered out to sea and blew itself out. Angry critics, thinking Pat Robertson was saying God had given him magical powers, responded. "Man has never been able to control the weather. Who does this man think he is, saying his prayers and the prayers of his viewers actually caused a hurricane to change its course?"

There is precedent, however. Such miracle stories abound in the Bible. Moses held out his rod over the waters of the Red Sea and they parted. Joshua, needing more daylight to finish his battle against the combined armies of the Amorites, commanded "the sun to stand still." But it's the story of Jesus' authority over the wind and waves that gives us the best insight into God's miracles over nature.

> *That day, when evening came* (Jesus had been teaching up in the northern area of Israel), *He said to His disciples, "Let us go over to the other side." Leaving the crowd behind, they took Him along, just as He was, in the boat. There were also other boats with Him.*

The story begins near Capernaum, on the north coast of the Sea of Galilee, a large, inland lake. The lake is surrounded on three sides by high mountains. The south side is bordered by a plain and opens into a deep valley through which the Jordan River flows into the Dead Sea—the lowest place on the surface of the earth. The Golan Heights, to the north and east, are mountains which fall off steeply into the lake. These mountains are laced with canyons, called wadis, which empty toward the water. When wind from the north or east blows through these canyons, it has the affect of a wind tunnel, causing the water of the lake to become turbulent. If the wind blows from the west, over the top of Mount Arbel which towers 2000 feet above the lake near Tiberias, it has an equally strong turbulent effect.

It was after sundown when Jesus finished His teaching near Capernaum, on the northern coast. He then got into the open fishing boats with His friends and asked them to take Him to the other side of the lake—a distance of about 13 miles. A furious squall came up, and the waves broke over the boat so that it was nearly swamped. Jesus was in the stern sleeping on a cushion. The disciples woke Him, shouting, "Teacher, don't you care if we drown?" He got up, rebuked the wind and said to the waves, "Quiet! Be still!" Then the wind died down and was completely calm.

Ordinarily after such a storm it takes the sea a long time to grow calm. But in this case, the sea was instantly calm. When Jesus speaks a word, not only does the storm cease, but the effects of it, all the remains of it, disappear as well.

The words that He uses in speaking to the waves are the identical words He used in Mark 1:25 when He spoke to a man possessed of a demon. "Be quiet! Shut up!" Now He uses these words to speak to the wind and waves. Standing up in the stern of the wildly rocking boat, He looks at the sky and sea and shouts, "Shut up and sit down!" Instantly the wind ceases to blow and the sea grows calm. Then, turning to His disciples, He gently rebukes them also.

"Why are you so afraid? Do you still have no faith?"

"Who is this man?" the disciples ask. "Even the wind and the waves obey Him."

Jesus said what He had just done was done by "faith." He indicates the disciples could have done the same thing if they had faith.

There are basically two kinds of miracles. There are those miracles which happen because God Himself intervenes. No prayer, no faith, no human agent is involved. God simply overrides a law of nature because He sees what needs to take place and there is no man there to do it.

Other miracles involve man. In these, man is the agent God uses to bring the miracles to pass. When man is involved, faith becomes a major factor. What is faith? Faith is simply believing God is in charge and has given to man all the dominion He gave to Jesus.

Man has dominion over the things of this world because Christ is in him. Jesus was, and is, the Living God. When He comes into us in the person of His Holy Spirit, He brings with Him all His power and authority. To the Colossian Christians Paul pointed out that "Christ in you is the hope of glory" (cf. Colossians 1:27). He went ahead to say, "You have been given fullness in Christ, who is the head over every power and authority" (Colossians 2:10). In short, all the power and dominion of Jesus resides in us.

What is the power and dominion which resides in Jesus?

The night before He was crucified Jesus told His disciples, "I tell you the truth, anyone who has faith in Me will do what I have been doing" (John 14:12). What had He been doing? He had been healing the sick, casting out demons, and taking authority over nature. He went on to further challenge His followers by saying, "He (those who believe in Jesus) will do even greater things than these, because I am going to the Father. And I will do whatever you ask in My name, so that the Son may bring glory to the Father. You may ask Me for anything in My name, and I will do it" (John 14:12-14).

Followers of Jesus across the centuries have been confused by the meaning of "the name of Jesus." When Jesus tells us to pray in His name, He is not referring to the closing words of a prayer which says "In Jesus' name, Amen." He is talking about recognizing Him for who He is, His power, His dominion. The little formula, "In the name of Jesus" is meaningless unless we recognize who He is, that He is in us.

It is Jesus' dominion over all things—including nature—which gave Him the authority to stand up in the boat and say to nature, "I'm going to override you. I am in charge here. You, natural law, you wind and waves, hear Me! Your boss, your creator is speaking! I'm telling you to change, to stop this, to be calm, to sit down and to shut up." He says it to demons, and He says it to the sea. Both obey Him.

Who is this man? Paul explains in a dissertation to the Christians in Rome. "Therefore, just as sin entered the world through one man, and death through sin, and in this way death came to all men, because all sinned—for before the law was given sin was in the world. But sin is not taken into account when there is no law" (Romans 5:12-13).

Sin is the mentality that causes us to say,"I am going to do things my way rather than God's way." Sin, then, is rebellion against God. It is caused by lack of faith. You cannot have sin and faith at the same time, because sin and faith are opposites. Faith is believing that God is, that He is good, and that He wants to work through you. Sin is rebellion against God and His plan, saying, "God is not who He says He is. I can't trust Him, I can't believe Him. I'm going to do things my way."

Jesus came to earth to overcome sin. His presence re-establishes our belief in God. He brings us back to God. Atonement, which is what Jesus does, (He atones for our sin) is a bridge between man in his sin, and God in His holiness. Jesus is our atonement. He bridges that gap so we can understand who God is. In Romans 5, Paul says sin came into the world through Adam. Now we all are infected with it. We've lost the ability to believe. Traces of faith are found in the hearts of little children, but the older we grow the more the systems of this world work on our sinful nature until, left alone, we totally rebel against God.

Paul goes ahead to say that Adam "was a pattern of the one to come" (Romans 5:14).

What did Adam have, in the Garden, before he sinned? He had dominion. He was in charge of this earth: the animals, nature, everything. God put him there to tend the Garden, and gave him total dominion. "Adam, it's yours. You are in charge." He ruled the earth. He was king of all the earth. Everything on the earth was under his charge. He had total dominion over everything. Thus, when he said, "I think I'll go one step beyond," we see his foolishness. He didn't know what he had, because he had never lost it. You don't realize what you have until it's taken away. Only then are you able to look back and say, "Oh, God, I wish I had that back." That is the remorse and regret of sin. Adam was given total dominion over all the earth. He had the ability to speak to the wind and the waves, and to say, "Quiet! Be still!" Dominion means being god of this world. But Adam lost that through sin. Instead of occupying the place of lord of the earth, instead of being the genuine article, he became simply the "pattern of the one to come."

Commenting on this, Paul says, "For as in Adam all die, so in Christ all will be made alive" (1 Corinthians 15:22). Then he concludes, "The first man Adam became a living being, the last Adam, a life-giving spirit" (1 Corinthians 15:45). God gave Jesus the same dominion He gave Adam in the Garden. Now Jesus has passed that along to all those who welcome Him as Lord of their lives. Jesus said to His followers, "That which is Mine, I give to you. It's yours. It's not just for Me." Do you know who believes this? Little kids. They are able to believe because they have not grown up in a world that is filled with pride and humanistic knowledge.

When something happens to me, when the wind blows across my lake and there are waves in my life, I go find a little kid to pray for me. I don't want someone praying for me who is filled with worldly knowledge. I want someone who believes, someone who is willing to claim the power of Jesus as given and walk it out. That's the reason Jesus said if you want to enter the Kingdom of Heaven, you will have to come as a little child.

That's not to say that we should get rid of all worldly knowledge. It simply means we should not lean on our own understanding.

When Jesus stood and rebuked the waves, all He did was exert His natural being—that which had been promised in prophecy and which was intended for all believers. "But at Your rebuke the waters fled, at the sound of Your thunder they took to flight" (Psalm 104:7). Although in this psalm David was talking about the creation process, that creation power—the power of the Creator over nature—remained evident in God's Son. Now His natural being was also supernatural, because He was not tainted by sin as we are tainted by sin. For us to have this same power we, as adults, must go through a process. Jesus was born—and remained—sinless. By that the Bible means He never doubted nor disobeyed God. Therefore, when He was faced with a situation which was hindering the will of God, it was natural for Him to take authority. Jesus was living in dominion.

It was never for His own benefit. He never changed a camel into a Cadillac. He never even changed the rocks into bread so He could have something to eat. The night He was arrested He could have called the angels (who were at His beck and call) to protect Him from the soldiers. Instead, He submitted Himself to God's higher plan—the plan of the cross. His miracles were for one purpose only—for the glory of God. He never profited a single time. Now the big questions is this: Is this kind of miracle for today, or are we simply at the mercy of those who report the weather without having authority over the weather? I give you three contemporary examples and let you decide for yourself.

In 1970, two years after I had entered the dimension of Spirit-led living, I received a call from the principal of the high school in the community where we live. He wanted me to preach the sermon to the graduating class at baccalaureate. The high school was new and had never had a baccalaureate service before, but since several of the graduating seniors attended our little church, they put pressure on the school administration which agreed. It was to be a big affair in the football stadium the first Sunday night in June.

I gave little thought to it, for we were having our own problems in the church about that time. We lived in a transient community and a number of our people were either associated with the nearby Kennedy Space Center or stationed at Patrick Air Force Base. As a result, people were constantly moving in and out of the community—more out than in. Our church had grown even smaller than the original 40 families we began with a year before, and now my open declaration that I had been "baptized in the Holy Spirit" had everyone on edge, wondering what was going to happen next. They were pleased that I had been asked to speak to the new, big high school, however, for they knew that at least 80 percent of the students were not Christians. They hoped I would be able to say something that would turn them to God.

They didn't know (nor did I) that it would come in the form of a demonstration—not a sermon.

Three days before the scheduled Sunday evening service in the football stadium, the east coast of Florida was buffeted by a preseason hurricane which came roaring through the Carribean and up the Atlantic seacoast until it reached our city of Melbourne. Mysteriously it remained stationary, about 10 miles off the coast, dumping tons of water on our city. It rained torrents for 48 hours straight. Sunday morning the high school principal called my house.

"We have almost three inches of water on the grass turf

at the stadium," he said. "If it doesn't stop raining by four o'clock this afternoon, we're calling off the baccalaureate service."

I went to church that morning in an anxious mood. Ordinarily I'm not too eager to speak at community functions, but this was different. For the first time in my life, I felt I had something to share with the young people—and their parents. But I couldn't do a thing unless the rain stopped. And with the eye of the hurricane directly off the coast, it seemed there was no way that it would stop. Even if the hurricane began to move, it would not be far enough away by evening for the rain to cease.

That afternoon I called five or six of the men in the congregation and asked them to meet me at the Tabernacle Church at 3:00 p.m. to pray. They sensed my urgency and agreed to be there. We arrived in the pouring rain and dashed to the shelter of the building. We stood in a circle at the side of the little meeting room and held hands. The rain was falling so hard we could scarcely make ourselves heard. One by one the men prayed.

"Lord, you control the weather. Please make the rain stop."

"Lord, you opened the Red Sea; now part the clouds so we can have the service tonight."

"Lord, Jamie can't speak in the rain. Isn't there something you can do about it?"

"Lord, if it be your will that the rain stop, we sure would appreciate it."

They were all good, honest, sincere prayers. But powerless. Nothing happened. In fact, I don't think we really expected anything to happen. We were just praying because we didn't know what else to do.

Then it was my turn. But when I opened my mouth, instead of the usual "if it be thy will" prayer, I heard myself shouting— not begging, but commanding. And I wasn't praying to God, I was taking authority over the elements.

"IN THE MIGHTY NAME OF JESUS, I COMMAND YOU, CLOUDS, GO AWAY! I COMMAND YOU, RAIN, STOP FALLING! I REBUKE YOU, EVIL HURRICANE, AND COMMAND YOU TO DEPART! OPEN, CLOUDS, AND LET THE SUN SHINE THROUGH!"

My word! Had that come out of me? I had never spoken like that before. I looked around at the other men, still standing in our circle holding hands. They were all staring at me—and I could understand why. None of us, including me, seemed to want to hang around any longer. I choked out, "Let's go home." We all picked up our raincoats and umbrellas and headed for the door.

But instead of walking out into the rain, we walked out into brilliant sunshine. Water was everywhere. The streets were flooded up over the curbs and sidewalks. Water was dripping from the trees and plants. But overhead the sky was blue and the summer sun shone through the clouds as they scudded for the safety of the horizon.

"Hallelujah!" one of the men shouted. Then, catching himself, he blushed. We dashed for our cars, but I knew something had happened in that room which would not only change my life forever, but change the lives of those men with me.

That night I could scarcely believe my eyes. The stands at the football field were full. The high school graduating class, dressed in caps and gowns, marched barefoot, sloshing through the standing water, to their chairs on the field. All around us we could see the rain falling in sheets. Lightning flashed in the eastern sky and thunder, angry and threatening, tried to scare us. But the football stadium was under clear skies. Overhead, beyond the bright lights, I could see the stars. The local Methodist pastor, who was to give the invocation, marched beside me as we sloshed through the water toward the platform in the middle of the field. "Aren't you going to carry your umbrella in case it starts to rain?"

he asked.

I'm sure he didn't understand my grin. "Knowing what I know, to carry an umbrella would be to deny what I've just seen. I'm a lot safer standing on the promises than sitting under an umbrella." I didn't speak long. Maybe I didn't want to test God too much. But I told the kids what had happened. I felt they had the right to know. I pointed to the rain clouds and told them God had promised just this small window of relief, and recommended they get back to their cars as quickly as possible when the service was over. But once under cover, they needed to remember God is a God of miracles—and they had just seen one.

As I was driving out of the parking lot it started to rain again—and continued to rain for another 24 hours before the hurricane moved out to sea and dissipated.

The idea that we have authority over the weather is foreign to us. But let's pause and consider: God did not set certain laws of the universe in motion, then step back out of the way. Rather, He has given us the same authority He gave Jesus to override these laws—when it is His will—so that His higher purpose may be accomplished.

In the incident on the Sea of Galilee, Satan used the weather (remember, he is the prince of the power of the air) to try to keep Jesus from "crossing over to the other side" as He said was His intention. He chose the occasion while Jesus was asleep to do this. Actually, he wanted to kill Jesus and all His disciples, for he is at heart a murderer. However, Jesus overrode Satan's use of the laws of nature by evoking the higher law of love. He needed to reach the other side because He was going to encounter a demon-possessed man in Gadara who desperately needed deliverance. In the end, after He had rebuked the wind and waves, Jesus rebuked His disciples by reminding them that they, too, had this authority. All they needed to do was take it.

There are numerous stories of this authority over nature in the Bible. In Acts 27-28 we find a similar incident. Paul, under arrest by the authorities, is on his way to Rome where he will be tried by Roman officials. Before leaving Crete Paul warns his captors, "Men, I can see that our voyage is going to be disastrous and bring great loss to ship and cargo, and to our own lives also" (Acts 27:10). Contrast this to the statement Jesus made to His disciples in Mark 4:35 when He said, "Let us go over to the other side." Jesus knew they were going to cross the Sea of Galilee safely. Paul knew a great storm was going to destroy their ship on the Mediterranean. In Paul's case, the military commander "instead of listening to Paul" (whose words came from God), "followed the advice of the pilot and of the owner of the ship." A hurricane swept down on them shortly after they set sail. The ship was driven hundreds of miles off course, and finally was smashed to pieces on the beach of the island of Malta.

If we have the authority to rebuke the wind and the waves, why didn't Paul do what Jesus did? It's not that Paul did not have authority over nature. He did, as is revealed in a remarkable incident that took place shortly after they were shipwrecked on the beach of Malta. Rather, God had given Paul insight into the future, just as He had given it to Jesus. Jesus knew they were to cross the Sea of Galilee to Gadara. He knew it was not time for Him or His disciples to die. God's method of preventing that was to give Jesus a word of knowledge concerning His (God's) plan, and to give Him authority to rebuke the storm.

The same thing happened in Paul's situation. Paul was given a word of knowledge that God did not intend for him or anyone else aboard the prison ship to perish at sea. He also informed Paul that this time it was His plan for the ship to be destroyed. Yet it is obvious God allowed the hurricane to drive the ship to near disaster on the beaches of Malta. As surely as He wanted Jesus to minister to the people in

Gadara, He wanted Paul to minister to the people of Malta. Thus we see that even though God gives us the power and authority to rebuke bad weather, He does not want us to rebuke all bad weather—just that which gets in the way of His purposes on earth. Paul's authority over nature was exhibited the night they were shipwrecked on the beach. The wet, cold sailors were greeted by friendly islanders who built a huge fire so they could dry out. Paul, warming himself by the fire, was suddenly bitten by a deadly carpet viper which slithered out of the burning brushwood. Instead of dying, however, he took authority over the fatal venom, threw the snake back into the fire, and suffered no ill effects. The islanders, amazed, sensed he had supernatural power. They took him to the chief official of the island who was gravely sick. Paul laid hands on him, prayed, and the man was healed. Following that, many other sick people came to him and were healed. The ship's crew and passengers remained on Malta three months and finally set sail for Rome where Paul lived for two years before his death.

How can we determine whether we should take authority over nature, as Jesus did in the boat and Paul did when the snake bit him, or whether we should let nature have its way, as Paul did in the midst of the hurricane? God never wants us to use one gift to the exclusion of all the other gifts of the Spirit. In several places Jesus said He did only what God told Him to do. Both Jesus and Paul had a word of knowledge from God. Jesus felt, in His heart, God wanted Him to rebuke nature. Paul knew God wanted the storm to accomplish another purpose—so he withheld his rebuke.

Could Paul have exerted his authority, spoken to the hurricane, and made it stop? That question comes close to being "idle speculation," but the answer is "no." Paul had authority to rebuke only what God wanted rebuked.

In another situation Paul complained that he had a "thorn in the flesh" that he had not only rebuked, but had begged

God to remove. But it remained. When he went back to God to determine why he did not have authority over this particular affliction, God told him He had a higher purpose. He was using the affliction (despite endless debate, not one today knows what it was) to teach him something he could not have learned otherwise: "My grace is sufficient for you, for My power is made perfect in weakness" (2 Corinthians 12:9).

Paul believed his affliction was "a messenger of Satan," giving us some indication it was not a physical problem, but perhaps a bad relationship, recurring memory, or even some kind of personal temptation which he just had to live with. Whatever it was, it was not deadly, just tormenting. On the other hand, there was no doubt the viper was sent from Satan to kill him. Paul's discernment worked instantly in that case. Perhaps he recalled the times John Mark had quoted Jesus' final words on earth: "Go into all the world and preach the good news to all creation. . . . and these signs will accompany those who believe: In My name they will drive out demons; they will speak in new tongues; they will pick up snakes with their hands; and when they drink deadly poison, it will not hurt them at all; they will place their hands on sick people, and they will get well" (Mark 16:15, 17-18). That was exactly what took place on Malta.

We have dominion over anything that interrupts the will and purpose of God in our lives, the will and purpose of God on earth.

One afternoon my wife and I were driving along the intercoastal waterway on the east coast of Florida. The highway runs right along the wide expanse of water called the Indian River, separated from the Atlantic Ocean by a narrow strip of land which runs most of the length of the state. Looking out over the water I spotted, several miles to the north, a giant water spout. A water spout is actually a tornado over water, its long gray funnel extending from the base of dark clouds and twisting down to the surface of the water. It seemed to be heading in our direction, right down the middle of the mile-wide lagoon.

"That's beautiful!" I remarked to my wife. All I could see in it was the rugged beauty of nature.

My wife, however, instantly had a word of knowledge from God. "It's not beautiful. It's wicked and evil and sent by Satan to destroy." Then, pointing through the windshield of the car at the water spout, she commanded in a loud voice, "I rebuke you in the name of Jesus!"

Instantly the water spout broke off from the base of the cloud. Within seconds we could see sky through the widening crack. It continued coming toward us down the waterway, but grew smaller and smaller. I pulled the car over to the side of the road and we waited, watching. The water spout, now only a few feet high, came right into the shallow water next to the road where we were parked, swirled the water, shrank down until it was only inches high, then fizzled out—leaving only ripples.

It was the same experience I once had with a mortally wounded rattlesnake I had shot. The snake turned to attack me. When it was just a few feet away, it drew back its head to strike, but life was already gone, and it fell dead at my feet. The water spout now fell dead at our feet. But in this case, my wife had not used a gun—she had used spiritual authority.

Certain things in nature are evil. Poison is evil. Deadly snakes are evil. Cancer—cells in rebellion against their Creator—is evil. As Lucifer and his angels, who now make up the evil empire of Satan and his demons, rebelled against God and were thrown out of heaven, so cancer is composed of cells which rebel against God. While God may function wonderfully in the hearts of cancer-stricken patients, I believe cancer is always evil and God wants us to take authority over it.

We have dominion over all things that prevent us from being the people of God. The problem is, we don't take it. We don't take it because we don't believe God. We don't believe it when He says, "I want you to be healthy, I want you to be happy, I want you to be prosperous. I want you to live at peace with My creation." We don't believe God wants us to be joyful, therefore we live in our misery, rather than taking dominion over the source of our unhappiness.

We have dominion in Christ; but we must take dominion over this world. All we need to do is hear God, and once having heard Him, take authority. Even the wind and the waves will obey the man or woman who takes dominion in the name of Jesus.

Jerry Woodfill, a scientist with NASA, was the project engineer responsible for Apollo warning systems. Later he became NASA's Orbiter Experiment Data Manager. On April 13, 1970, while monitoring the third lunar expedition, Apollo 13, he was at his position at the Space Center in Houston when he heard the words coming back from the moon: "Houston, we've had a problem." An oxygen tank in the spacecraft had exploded!

Looking at his console he realized the alarm system he had helped design indicated five or six different situations—any one of which could mean the astronauts would not return to earth alive. They had run out of electrical power; there weren't enough filters to clean the carbon dioxide out of the cabin; and most precarious—there was a hurricane at their landing site. Unknown to Jerry, people around the world heard the news and began to pray. One by one, Jerry said, he saw five technical miracles occur that no one could explain.

But the last and greatest need, however, remained. It was the one man could do nothing about. The weather. The hurricane in the Atlantic Ocean was growing in intensity—as though it was controlled by an evil power determined to destroy the lives of the men coming back from the moon. To change the landing site could mean the Apollo spacecraft, and its occupants, would be lost.

The re-entry officer at the Space Center turned to the chief meteorologist. "What do you think?"

The weatherman answered, "You'd better change the landing site or they'll land in the hurricane."

Then the re-entry officer did a strange thing. "No," he said. "I'm going to ignore your advice. Something tells me I ought to bring it down right where I intended."

Even as the Apollo 13 spacecraft streaked toward the eye of the hurricane, the great storm suddenly turned course—as if being pushed by a giant hand—and unexpectedly and inexplicably moved hundreds of miles north of the landing site. The space capsule splashed down right on target—in calm seas with sunny skies overhead.

Jerry was astonished. He had never seen so many things go right just when he needed them. Several weeks later he received a letter from a school teacher. The teacher wrote that her class of 14 mentally retarded children had been following the news of Apollo 13. The morning the astronauts left the moon and headed back toward earth one of the girls said, "Teacher, I heard on the radio that even if our astronauts should survive re-entry into earth atmosphere, they're going to land in a hurricane and be lost at sea."

The teacher, a Christian, replied, "Children, remember the story in the Bible about the terrible storm on the Sea of Galilee and how Jesus stretched forth His hand and calmed the sea?"

They nodded. She knew her school officials might discipline her if she actually led the children in prayer. She wisely continued, "I don't know about you, but at lunchtime when we say our noontime blessing, I'm going to be praying that the Lord Jesus will move that storm and calm the sea."

It was at that time, as the children were praying, that the

re-entry officer felt strongly impressed to make the decision to land the spacecraft in the original drop zone. And at that exact moment the giant hurricane suddenly rumbled into life and began its rapid exit from the area—leaving the sea calm and clear for the Apollo capsule to land safely.

Because of these miraculous incidents Jerry Woodfill began searching the Bible for answers. In its pages he discovered the God who controls nature, and who responds to simple faith, such as that exhibited by a class of mentally retarded children. A few weeks later Jerry attended a Saturday morning prayer breakfast and turned his life over to the lordship of Jesus Christ, who still calms storms and performs miracles.

Father, I know You want Your people to be people of dominion. Not only for their own sake, but for the benefit of Your creation. As with Adam and Eve, You want us to live in this creation, tending the garden, blessing that which is good, taking authority over that which is evil. I do not believe You want us to be at the mercy of germs, disease, muscular and nervous illnesses, the weather, evil things in nature, Satan or his demons. You have made us people of dominion. Give us the boldness to exert that which is ours already—in Jesus' name and for Your glory. Amen.

THREE

POWER OVER MANY DEMONS
Jesus Confronts a Maniac

"Go home to your family and tell them how much the Lord has done for you. . . ."

MARK 5:1-20
(also Matthew 8:28-34 and Luke 8:26-39)

They went across the lake to the region of the Gerasenes (Cadarenes). When Jesus got out of the boat, a man with an evil spirit came from the tombs to meet Him. This man lived in the tombs, and no one could bind him any more, not even with a chain. For he had often been chained hand and foot, but he tore the chains apart and broke the irons on his feet. No one was strong enough to subdue him. Night and day among the tombs and in the hills he would cry out and cut himself with stones.

When he saw Jesus from a distance, he ran and fell on his knees in front of Him. He shouted at the top of his voice, "What do you want with me, Jesus, Son of the Most High God? Swear to God that You won't torture me!" For Jesus was saying to him, "Come out of this man, you evil spirit!"

Then Jesus asked him, "What is your name?"

"My name is Legion," he replied, "for we are many."

And he begged Jesus again and again not to send them out of the area.

A large herd of pigs was feeding on the nearby hillside. The demons begged Jesus, "Send us among the pigs; allow us to go into them." He gave them permission, and the evil spirits came out and went into the pigs. The herd, about two thousand in number, rushed down the steep bank into the lake and were drowned.

Those tending the pigs ran off and reported this in the town and countryside, and the people went out to see what had happened. When they came to Jesus, they saw the man who had been possessed by the legion of demons, sitting there, dressed and in his right mind; and they were afraid. Those who had seen it told the people what had happened to the demon-possessed man—and told about the pigs as well. Then the people began to plead with Jesus to leave their region.

As Jesus was getting into the boat, the man who had been demon-possessed begged to go with Him. Jesus did not let him, but said, "Go home to your family and tell them how much the Lord has done for you, and how He has had mercy on you." So the man went away and began to tell in the Decapolis how much Jesus had done for him. And all the people were amazed.

Our concept of Jesus will always be distorted if we study His miracles apart from His teachings. Today there are many people who have discovered the secret of God's miracle-working power. They are using it to heal people and set them free from various bondages. That is good, and we should rejoice that it is happening. However, unless the miracles are viewed in the light of what Jesus taught, we will begin to believe that miracles are an end in themselves, that they are the only reason Jesus came to earth. That will invariably produce a lopsided ministry which will eventually topple.

In studying this particular event which took place early in the public ministry of Jesus, we need to keep in mind something He said at the close of His public ministry—actually His final recorded words before ascending to heaven. At that time, He said "All authority in heaven and on earth has been given to Me. Therefore go and make disciples of all nations, baptizing them in the name of the Father and of the Son and of the Holy Spirit, and teaching them to obey everything I have commanded you. And surely I will be with you always, to the very end of the age" (Matthew 28:18-20).

On the basis of that, we understand the authority that Jesus Christ possessed as the Son of God—authority over demons and authority to perform miracles—is given to each of us also. But we also understand that the reason for the use of this authority is to make disciples of others, which is the heart and meaning of evangelism. Evangelism is not only telling people about Jesus, it is demonstrating Jesus' authority through miracles and using those miracles to make disciples.

Several years after the resurrection, Paul traveled to Athens, Greece, to share the gospel. Standing on Mars Hill, he preached a deeply intellectual sermon on "The Unknown God." The people were impressed, but no one became a disciple. Discouraged, Paul left Athens and traveled to Corinth, during which time God convinced him he was taking the wrong approach to evangelism. When he reached Corinth, he corrected his mistake. Later, he reminded the Corinthians, "When I came to you, brothers, I did not come with eloquence or superior wisdom as I proclaimed to you the testimony about God. For I resolved to know nothing while I was with you except Jesus Christ and Him crucified. I came to you in weakness and fear, and with much trembling. My message and my preaching were not with wise and persuasive words, but with a demonstration of the Spirit's power, so that your faith might not rest on men's wisdom, but on God's power" (1 Corinthians 2:1-5).

Paul had learned that the purpose of miracles was to demonstrate the power of God so others might see, have faith in God, and become disciples.

With that in mind, we are better equipped to understand all that took place that evening and the next morning in this forlorn area on the southeastern shore of the Sea of Galilee. It was late afternoon, just at sundown, when Jesus and His disciples left Capernaum on the northern shore of the lake and headed south towards the region of the Decapolis—named after the ten cities in the area south of Galilee and east of where the lake empties into the Jordan River.

> *That day when evening came, He said to His disciples,*
> *"Let us go over to the other side."*

The Sea of Galilee is approximately 13 miles long and eight miles wide at its widest place. Crossing the lake from north to south, Jesus and His disciples had encountered a ferocious storm which had almost swamped their boats. Jesus had awakened, rebuked the storm (which responded instantly to his command), and the boats sailed on, landing on a remote beach on the southeast section of the lake, just a few miles east of the Jordan River.

It had been a strange night, beginning with what had all the earmarks of being a supernatural storm, sent by Satan for the intent purpose of killing Jesus. Landing on the shore of the region known as the Decapolis, the

disciples were frightened. This was foreign territory to
them. A Jew would rather go through Samaria than pass
through the Decapolis, for there was something intensely
evil about the entire region—a region ruled and inhabited
by demon forces.

Who and what are demons?
Paul says "our struggle is not against flesh and blood,
but against the rulers, against the authorities, against the
powers of this dark world and against the spiritual forces
of evil in the heavenly realms" (Ephesians 6:12).

Does that mean demons are real?
Absolutely!
The most powerful tactic of Satan is to convince spiritual
leaders that demons do not exist, allowing them to continue
their evil work without direct and authoritative interference
from the very ones God has appointed to combat them.
Jesus, however, never argued over the existence of demons
(sometimes called devils). He recognized their existence
because He was present with the Father at the Great
Council Table when the archangel, Lucifer, who at that
time was in charge of the music of the universe, tried
to assume full power over God. The story is told in vivid
detail in Revelation 12:7-9 and Isaiah 14:11-23. Isaiah
describes how—before the formation of the earth as we
know it—the chief musician, the archangel Lucifer,
attempted a coup against God. He said, "I will make myself
like the Most High" (Isaiah 14:14).

God's retribution was swift. Since angels were created
by God as immortal beings, His decision was to banish
Lucifer (known in the New Testament as Satan) from all
heavenly activity. "All your pomp has been brought down
to the grave, along with the noise of your harps" (Isaiah
14:11). From that time Satan was assigned to wander the
earth, earthbound. After his assault on God's newly created

beings, Adam and Eve, God intervened and assigned him an even lower level. "You will crawl on your belly and you will eat dust all the days of your life" (Genesis 3:14). He promised that the offspring of woman would "crush your head and you will strike his heal" (Genesis 3:15)—an obvious reference to the work of Christ. Finally, God told the Apostle John that when Jesus returns and sets up His Kingdom, the devil will be "thrown into the lake of burning sulfur" and will be "tormented day and night forever and ever" (Revelation 20:10).

John gives added detail. "And there was war in heaven. Michael and his angels fought against the dragon, and the dragon and his angels fought back. But he was not strong enough, and they lost their place in heaven. The great dragon was hurled down—that ancient serpent called the devil or Satan, who leads the whole world astray. He was hurled to the earth, and his angels with him" (Revelation 12:7-9).

Jesus, in a prelude to the revelation God would later give to John, mentioned this when He said the day would come when "the devil and his angels" would be cast into eternal fire (Matthew 25:41).

Lucifer, then, was not the only one banished from heaven, expelled with him was his vast retinue of angels. It is my theory that his group included a number of "little angels," those special beings which comprise the angelic force called cherubim and seraphim. Cherubim and seraphim have no authority of their own. They simply do the bidding of their angel. It is these cherubim and seraphim which make up the demon forces of Satan. Since they have no form, they are forced to take up habitation in living beings. Sometimes these demons possess animals, but usually they are assigned to humans.

While God seems to assign His own angels to various people and for various tasks, there is no biblical evidence

God puts angels on stationary assignment over geographical areas. (There is an ancient Jewish legend that certain angels have been assigned to the Mount Sinai region.) However, it is Satan, whose kingdom is this earth, who makes the major assignments over geographical areas. These assignments take place only when God's people abdicate their authority on earth, or when earthly rulers literally ask for or call in the rulers of darkness to reign over their territory.

The region of the Decapolis seemed to be such a place. Jesus only visited there twice. Both of His visits were short, barely overnight, and on both occasions He encountered strange manifestations of Satan. This place was, indeed, Satan's territory, inhabited by countless demons.

Decapolis literally means "the Ten Cities." The area in which these cities were located was on the east side of the Jordan River and south of the Sea of Galilee, in what is now the nation of Jordan. (One of them, Scythopolis, was on the west side of the river.) The cities were essentially Greek. Their names: Pella, Dion, Gerasa, Philadelphia, Raphana, Kanatha, Hippos, Damascus (not to be confused with the capital of Syria much farther north), and Gadara. Originally, these cities had been part of Syria, but operated much as the ancient Greek city-states with their own coinage and government. They associated for mutual defense but remained semi-independent until the middle of the second century B.C. when they were captured by the Jewish Maccabees.

When the Romans, under Pompey, conquered the Jews, they restored these ten cities to a strange independence. Since Rome ruled the Middle East with a system of tributary kings, they could give these cities little protection. The cities banded together against Jewish encroachment. They remained stubbornly Greek, worshiping Greek gods. The only Jews who came here were apostates, Jews who had renounced their Judaism for the sensual and satanic life of the Greeks. The Jews of Jesus' day believed the Decapolis was the geographical headquarters of Satan and his demons. Many who have studied the patterns of Satan and his demons believe there are certain regions, certain cities, which are ruled by powerful demonic forces. These are areas which, for one reason or another, have been turned over to Satan by the inhabitants. The ancient cities of Sodom and Gomorrah, on the western shore of the Dead Sea, for example, had been given over to powerful, satanic rulers of the underworld. Abraham's nephew, Lot, had gone there to live after failing as a shepherd and squandering the inheritance of the green Jordan Valley given him by his uncle. When God told Abraham He was going to destroy the two cities because of their gross wickedness, Abraham pleaded with God to spare the cities. God said He would spare them if Abraham could find ten righteous men in the two cities. He searched, but was unable to find ten good men—so great was the power of the underworld rulers (Genesis 18:16-19:29).

Many years later the prophet Daniel, sitting in exile in ancient Babylon, a huge city located on a site 40 miles south of modern Baghdad, Iraq, began praying intensely. For three weeks his prayers went unanswered. But on the twenty-fourth day of fasting and praying, he had a visitation from an angel. "Do not be afraid, Daniel," the angel said. "Since the first day that you set your mind to gain understanding and to humble yourself before your God, your words were heard, and I have come in response to them. But *the prince of the Persian kingdom resisted me 21 days.* Then Michael, one of the chief princes, came to help me, because I was detained there with the king of Persia. Now I have come to explain to you what will happen to your people in the future, for the vision concerns a time yet to come" (Daniel 10:12-14).

Who was this "prince of the Persian kingdom"? Obviously, he was no small demon, but rather a powerful, dark angel assigned to a geographical area of the world called Persia. So great was his power, so strong his influence, even the normal angels (those heavenly beings used by God to bring supernatural messages to His people) could not get through. In this case the messenger (the Greek word angelos, "angel," means "messenger") needed help from the great archangel, Michael, to combat the demonic ruler of Persia.

Ancient Persia is now known as Iran, and remains one of the seats of demonic power in the world. Despite the little pockets of Christian witness still found in the nation, few places in the world exhibit the presence and power of Satan as much as the modern nation of Iran.

World travelers tell of discerning such spiritual rulers in various regions and cities of the world. I remember the sensation I had flying into Prague, Czechoslovakia, some years ago. As the Russian airliner let down through the clouds over what used to be one of the most beautiful cities in the world, I was suddenly aware of a great evil hovering over the city. This city, once renowned as the home of men like Good King Wenceslaus and Bible translator John Hus, had been given over to Satan by its rulers. Even though there are thousands of believers living and witnessing in Prague (which is the reason, I am certain, God has withheld His judgment), the chief ruler of that city is a dark angel appointed by Satan with the permission of the city rulers.

How can the bondage of these spiritual overlords be broken?

Several years ago the Tidewater area of Virginia was under this same kind of Satanic rule. It had become the proud home of some of the world's greatest occult leaders. Edgar Cayce had established his occult headquarters in the region. Virginia Beach, in particular, was well known as the home of many witches, Satanists, and occultists. The few churches in the area were all struggling against great odds. The "ruler of the kingdom of the air" (Ephesians 2:2) seemed in firm control.

In the early 1960s Pat Robertson chose Portsmouth, Virginia, in the Tidewater area, as the home for the Christian Broadcasting Network—the first Christian broadcasting network in history. Although dealing primarily with television, Pat's intention was to take spiritual dominion over an area which for many years had been ruled by an angel of Satan. He literally invaded the realm of Satan using a method of warfare which involved a strong base of praying people—people who agreed to pray daily, taking authority over Satan and his demons. He began by asking for 700 people who would agree to pray daily. He called these special people "The 700 Club"—the banner still flying over the flagship program of CBN. He also determined to expand the perimeters of his broadcast to the extreme borders of the Tidewater area—from the Atlantic ocean across the Chesapeake Bay and down into the Great Dismal Swamp of Virginia. He was bearding the lion in his den by taking over the airwaves for Christian television and radio.

Robertson took his cue from God's promise to Joshua. "I will give you every place where you set your foot . . . No one will be able to stand up against you all the days of your life . . . be strong and courageous, because you will lead these people to inherit the land I swore to their forefathers to give them. . . ." (Joshua 1:3, 5, 6). Robertson believed God had given America to the believers. The first permanent settlers had landed at Cape Henry, down river from Jamestown, less than 10 miles from where the present CBN headquarters are located. They had fasted, prayed, and planted a cross on the beach, claiming the new world for Jesus. Across the years, however, the leaders of the nation—and in particular, the spiritual leaders in the very area where the first claim was made—had turned the territory over to Satan. Robertson believed God had called him to take it back. It took almost 20 years, but today the CBN headquarters, featuring America's largest free-standing graduate school, CBN University, sits in the middle of Virginia Beach. And not only has Pat Robertson moved up to a greater sphere of spiritual influence, but some of the nation's strongest churches now flourish in the Tidewater area. The occult influence has waned to a mere shadow.

> *They went across the lake to the region of the Gaderenes. When Jesus got out of the boat, a man with an evil spirit came from the tombs to meet Him.*

There is some confusion about the location of this story, and about the number of men involved. Matthew says there were two demon-possessed men who approached Jesus. Mark speaks of only one. However, he does not rule out there was another; he just focuses in on one of them. Also, while Mark says Jesus landed in the region of the "Gerasenes," the ancient manuscripts of the three Gospel accounts also say it could have been the region of the Gadarenes. Gerasa can hardly be right since the only Gerasa was 36 miles inland from the lake. Gadara, on the other hand, is only six miles from the lake and does lie, as all accounts say, in the region known as the Decapolis.

Gadara is in limestone country. In the daytime it is a beautiful area made up of soft hills that have been eroded by centuries of wind and storms. The hills contain a number of caves, carved by wind and water, which the people of the area used for tombs.

Underground burial is very difficult in Israel. The soil is rocky. Digging a hole, especially a hole deep enough to bury a body, is a major task. One option for the Jews of Jesus' day was to lay the body on the ground and cover it with rocks to prevent predators from devouring it. These graves were often whitewashed for appearance' sake, giving rise to Jesus' charge that the Pharisees were "whitewashed tombs, which look beautiful on the outside but on the inside are full of dead men's bones" (Matthew 23:27).

The other option was to wrap the body in a shroud, like a mummy, and lay it in a cave. Such bodies were not embalmed, which was an Egyptian custom, but covered with spices to alleviate the stench of decaying flesh.

It was to such a graveyard Jesus came.

Graveyards were always apart from human habitation, partly for sanitary reasons, partly because Jewish law said "anyone who touches a human bone or a grave will be unclean for seven days" (Numbers 19:16). At the best of times this graveyard, located in the middle of Satan's territory, was an eerie place. After dark it must have been terrifying.

Aside from the genuine existence of demons, there was much superstition which abounded in Jewish folklore— even as we have our own "old wives' tales." Male demons were called *shedim*, and the female species, *lilin*. The Egyptians said the human body had 36 different parts, and every part could be occupied by a demon. They believe demons entered primarily by lurking beside a man as he ate so they could settle on his food. Thus, elaborate blessings were used to exorcise demons from food. Demons, it was said, were especially active in the nighttime before cockcrow. The disciples must have been terrified, after the encounter with the storm where all nearly drowned, to find Jesus wanting to visit a cemetery in demon-country after dark.

> *This man lived in the tombs, and no one could bind*
> *him anymore, not even with a chain. For he had often*
> *been chained hand and foot, but he tore the chains apart*
> *and broke the irons on his feet. No one was strong enough*
> *to subdue him. Night and day among the tombs and*
> *in the hills he would cry out and cut himself with stones.*

The small group of men were carefully making their way through the tombs, looking fearfully in all directions, perhaps more afraid to stay with the boat than to accompany Jesus through the haunted graveyard. Suddenly, leaping from behind a pile of rocks, was a wild man. Screaming like a banshee, he ran toward them, broken chains hanging from his wrists and ankles, his arms flailing, his hair flying behind him. He was totally naked—his body dripping with blood where he had deliberately cut himself with sharp stones.

Of all the scenes of the Bible, this one is the most terrifying.

Satan, it seems, has the power to give people supernatural strength. This man had been judged too dangerous to live among men. Mad men, people with mental illnesses, demon-possessed men—all were locked up in ancient days. This man, with maniacal strength, had broken the chains that held his wrists and ankles to some dungeon wall and had been driven into the tombs, the haunt of other demons. Yet Jesus never backed away as the man came rushing at them out of the night.

> *When he saw Jesus from a distance, he ran and fell*
> *on his knees in front of Him. He shouted at the top*
> *of his voice, "What do you want with me, Jesus, Son*
> *of the Most High God? Swear to God that You won't*
> *torture me!" For Jesus was saying to him, "Come out*
> *of this man, you evil spirit."*

While this man ordinarily ran at intruders with rage, he ran at Jesus with reverence. The spirit of the man desperately wanted help, causing him to fall on his knees at Jesus' feet. All the while the demons were shrieking and yelling, as if a beekeeper had plugged the outlets and then shaken the beehive.

Yet the demons, themselves, were forced to recognize Jesus for who He was. They called Him *Elion*, "Most High God"—the term reserved for Jehovah alone. If you need proof that Jesus is the Messiah, ask a demon. James says, "You believe that there is one God. Good! Even the demons believe that—and shudder" (James 2:19). Demons know who God is, and they recognize His Son.

It is clear Jesus made more than one attempt to set the man free. Verse eight says Jesus began by using His usual method—an authoritative order for the demon to come out. But nothing happened. Perhaps they did not hear because of the horrible noise they were making through the man. For whatever reason, Jesus continued His confrontation demanding of them, "What is your name?"

The fact Jesus commanded these demons to name themselves does not constitute a formula to be used by all who practice deliverance. It is simply the method Jesus used at this time and this place. On other occasions He used other methods—always listening to His Father and doing only what God told Him to do.

From the onset, however, this was a one-sided battle. These were the little guys taking on the Son of God. They knew, from the beginning, they were defeated. Suddenly their little territory, where they had ruled and reigned for centuries, was invaded by the Messiah.

It is difficult, as we read the account in the Bible, to distinguish who is speaking to Jesus—the demons or the man. The demons cry out, "Jesus, Son of the Most High

God," and the man cries, "Don't torture me." Demons are not afraid of torture. That's of no concern to them. But the man himself would be deathly afraid. He had been tortured before, evidenced by the chains.

Perhaps his concern was that Jesus was going to release him from the demons. He may have looked upon that as torture. Many people, having lived with their demons over a period of years, don't want to be released. It would mean taking on an entirely new lifestyle. Letting the demons control them, they believe, is far easier than being controlled by the Holy Spirit.

I have been around people who were dying of alcoholism, but their cry was, "Please don't take my bottle away from me! I can't live without it. That would be the worst of all tortures."

I have been around people suffocating to death from emphysema, who nevertheless listened to the demons and—between gasps—continued to chain-smoke cigarettes. To take their cigarettes away, they believed, would be torture.

It's possible the man Jesus encountered in the graveyard was a man afraid of wholeness. Yet there was a battle taking place between the mind and the heart—the battle that goes on inside of every one of us. The heart caused the man to rush to Jesus. The mind caused him to back off and say, "Don't torture me. Leave me alone." Part of him was rushing toward Jesus and the other part was pulling back. It's the perennial struggle with God. A part of us is saying, "Help me, O Lord," and the other part, clashing, cries, "Don't touch me." Unless settled, such a conflict will make madmen out of all of us.

There was another instance in the Bible where Jesus had to come back a second time to set a man free. It happened in Bethsaida with a blind man who only received partial sight when Jesus touched him. He returned for a second touch (Mark 8:22-26). His partial healing was not due to a lack of power in Jesus. Rather, it had to do with the man's will. God never forces us against our will. God waits until our will is ready to be subdued to His will. Then He acts.

The wild man didn't want to be set free. That was evidenced by his statement, "Don't torture me." Any person who genuinely wants to be set free from demon possession can be delivered. In fact, oftentimes just saying, "I want to be set free," brings the release. But when a person does as this man did, there is always a huge struggle.

In this case the demons, hiding behind the man's will, were able to fight back. They were tenacious, yet fearful, for they knew they had met their match.

When Jesus asked, "What is your name?" He was not talking to the man. He was speaking to the devils themselves.

> "My name is legion," he replied, "for we are many." And he begged Jesus again and again not to send them out of the area.

The Roman army was composed of large units, such as the modern regiment, called legions. The standard legion was made up of 6,000 men. Rome had 25 legions in her total army. Each legion was subdivided into 10 small units, called cohorts, consisting of 600 men each. The leader of these individual groups was called a tribune. The next level was a sixfold division of a cohort—a group of 100 men. This body was appropriately called a century and was commanded by a centurion. Rome had assigned five cohorts, or 3,000 soldiers, to the region of Judea. That meant this man had twice as many demons as the Romans had troops in Israel. Even so, this huge army of demons was no match against the Son of God, whom all God's angels worship (Hebrews 1:6). "He became as much superior to the angels as the name He has inherited is superior to theirs" (Hebrews 1:4).

The demons' greatest fear was banishment from the area where their overlord had assigned them—the area of the Decapolis. Luke says, "They begged Him repeatedly not to order them to go into the Abyss" (Luke 8:31). The word "Abyss" is capitalized in the original language. It does not refer to the cliff above the sea or one of the nearby wadis. They were begging: "Don't send us back to hell."

If we understood the nature of demons, we would understand how much authority we have over them. They are tortured, miserable creatures. I feel demons are fallen seraphim and cherubim who, after enjoying all the bliss of heaven, followed their leader into hell. They are tortured. They are out of place. They don't belong where they are. These miserable creatures now wreak their misery on everybody, as they take up residence here and there. Even as God's ministering angels make people happy, so these demon forces take up residence and make people miserable. They are under a tyrant, a lying ruler who has absolutely no good within him. He treats his employees just as poorly as he mistreats his customers. He is just as hard on his demons as he is on all the rest of us. They are frightened, forsaken creatures, doomed to wander and create mischief until they are thrown into the lake of fire with their master at the end of time. Knowing they were going to have to leave this man who had earlier allowed them to take residence in him, they now pleaded, asking Jesus not to send them back to Lucifer for reassignment.

A large herd of pigs was feeding on a nearby hillside. The demons begged Jesus, "Send us among the pigs;

*allow us to go into them." He gave them permission,
and the evil spirits came out and went into the pigs.
The herd, about two thousand in number, rushed down
the steep bank into the lake and were drowned.*

One might ask, what were pigs doing in Israel? Why
would Jews be raising pork when the animals were
considered unclean by kosher law? But this area was not
Jewish. The Decapolis was Greek. The only Jews who lived
there were apostate. When Jesus commanded the demons
to leave, the pigs couldn't handle them any better than
the man. Screaming and snorting, they stampeded over
the edge of the cliff and into the sea far below. There
is a bit of Jewish humor here in that Jesus seems to be
saying, "I might as well clean up this whole mess while
I'm here." In so doing, He not only got rid of the demons,
He got rid of the pigs at the same time.

*Those tending the pigs ran off and reported this in
the town and countryside, and the people went out to
see what had happened.*

When did this happen? Probably the next morning when
the swine-herders came through the cemetery and asked
the disciples if they had seen a herd of pigs. With a little
smile, the Jewish disciples just pointed over the cliff. The
herders, seeing the bloated bodies of their herd floating
in the water below, ran into town. Within the hour the
townspeople had raced to the scene to see for themselves.

*When they came to Jesus, they saw the man who had
been possessed by the legion of demons, sitting there,
dressed and in his right mind; and they were afraid.
Those who had seen it told the people what had happened
to the demon-possessed man—and told about the pigs*

*as well. Then the people began to plead with Jesus to
leave their region.*

How could the fate of the pigs be compared with the
fate of a man's soul? There is, even today, a cheap
sentimentalism which causes people to object to the
sacrifice of animals to save the lives of people. Whole
groups of people object to the use of rats in a research
laboratory where medicines are developed which save
countless lives. That is not to say we should be heartless
when it comes to God's creatures; it simply means we
should have a sense of godly priorities when it comes
to animal life over the lives—and souls—of human beings.

When you invite Christ into your life, all kinds of things
have to go. When we invite Him into a region, there are
certain things which must leave. It costs. Someone asks,
"Who paid for the pigs?" That was of no concern to Jesus.
He hadn't destroyed the farmer's pigs. That had been done
by the demons. Losing your pigs is one of the risks you
take when you choose to raise your animals in Satan's
territory. There is a price that goes with the presence of
Christ.

One would have thought the people of the area would
have been overjoyed to see this man delivered—not only
for his sake, but for their safety as well. However, since
the area was largely dependent on that huge herd of swine
for its economic stability, and since Jesus had come along
and upset everything, saying, in essence, their economic
base was wrong, they wanted Him to leave. Immediately.
Their routine of life had been terribly upset and they
wanted the disturbing element removed as quickly as
possible. As Matthew Henry once commented, "They
wanted his room rather than his company."

It is the age-old cry of the comfortable: "Don't disturb
me."

There is a lot of talk about the things life owes us. The godly man, however, knows life owes him precisely nothing. In fact, we owe life everything. If we think life owes us something, then we have no conscience about cheating on our taxes, stealing another's goods, even taking another's spouse—or his life. But when we realize we are "bought with a price," that the One who gave up the glory of Heaven literally purchased, with His life, our salvation, then we spend the rest of our lives returning, rather than stealing; giving, rather than getting; giving thanks when another is blessed (even at the expense of our pigs), rather than complaining.

Mark makes an interesting point about this man. In his narrative, Luke points out that "for a long time this man had not worn clothes" (Luke 8:27). Mark adds that the next morning, when the townspeople came trooping out to see the destruction, they found the man "dressed and in his right mind."

Not only had he been set free of the demon possession, but something had happened to his demeanor. He had decided to put his clothes on.

Some years ago I agreed to make a nationwide media tour, promoting one of the books I had written. In three weeks I visited 19 cities and was interviewed on 102 radio and television stations. On several occasions I visited two cities in one day, doing the morning shows in Phoenix, for instance, and the afternoon and evening progams in San Diego.

When I got to Los Angeles, I was exhausted. One of the radio stations which had scheduled me was north of the city. When I arrived I discovered it was owned and operated by Playgirl, a pornography firm which publishes magazines for women. The program was a one hour radio interview to begin at 3:00 p.m.

I almost backed out, but I was too tired to fight and

went on into the studio. The manager introduced me to
the young woman who was to conduct the interview. She
was a beautiful, six foot tall woman with long, red hair.
She was wearing a see-through, mesh blouse, and no
brassiere. Moments later I was seated across a small table
from her, with the radio microphone between us. I had
no choice but to stare at her nakedness.

I started to object. Then I asked myself, "What would
Jesus do in this situation?" I determined He would love
her, feel sad that she felt compelled to display herself
immodestly, and talk about miracles. Which is exactly what
I did.

About a third of the way through the interview, the young
woman, who seemed fascinated over the miracle stories
I was relating, reached down and picked up the clipboard
that held her interview notes. Instead of reading from
it, she held it over her chest for the remainder of the
interview. I had accepted her for what she was but as
I talked about God, she felt uneasy (as did Eve) with her
nakedness. The Holy Spirit, working through my testimony,
had convicted her that she needed to do what the former
wild man did—get dressed.

> As Jesus was getting into the boat, the man who
> had been demon-possessed begged to go with Him. Jesus
> did not let him, but said, "Go home to your family
> and tell them how much the Lord has done for you,
> and how He has had mercy on you." So the man went
> away and began to tell in the Decapolis how much Jesus
> had done for him. And all the people were amazed.

The man, naturally, wanted to go with Jesus. He wanted
to become one of His disciples. Jesus had another plan,
however. The man was to become a witness for Jesus Christ.
Earlier, Jesus had told some of His disciples if they would

lay down their fishermen's nets and follow Him, He would make them fishers of men. With this man, however, Jesus broke the pattern. Instead of being a disciple, Jesus wanted him to be a witness. He was to be a living, walking, unquestionable demonstration of the miracle power of Jesus Christ. Every place this man went, he would be known as a miracle—and no one can argue with a miracle.

Second, this was Jesus' first contact with Greek civilization. Perhaps that was the reason Jesus was so adamant about visiting the Decapolis. Even though He had limited knowledge while He resided in a human body, He surely knew, in His spirit, that the Jews would eventually reject the gospel—and it would be picked up by the Greeks and spread throughout the world. How significant that the glory of all Christianity which flowered in the Greek mind began with a man who had been possessed by demons.

Ancient legend has it that a Greek merchant from Decapolis, who dealt with textiles and purple dye, heard the miracle story from this unnamed man. In his travels back to Greece, he told the story to other merchants. One of them was a wealthy merchant in Philippi, a woman by the name of Lydia. The story was undoubtedly distorted by the time it reached her, but something happened in her heart and she yearned to know more about this Jesus and His Father, whom she began to love from afar.

Twenty years later, a small, apostolic band of missionaries, led by Paul and Silas, arrived at the Asia Minor port of Troas. Paul wanted to go north, to Turkey and Russia. However, Luke tells us that they "were kept by the Holy Spirit from preaching the word in the province of Asia. When they came to the border of Mysia, they tried to enter Bithynia, but the Spirit of Jesus would not allow them to" (Acts 16:6-7). That night, in a dream, Paul saw a man from Greece "standing and begging, come over to Macedonia (Greece) and help us" (Acts 16:9).

They embarked immediately, arrived in the Greek city of Philippi (which was under Roman dominion), and on the Sabbath went down to the river hoping to find a quiet place to pray. A crowd of women who were washing clothes (this would never have been permitted on the Sabbath in a Jewish community) gathered around the men as they began talking about Jesus. One of the women was Lydia, who instantly knew who they were talking about. She became the first Greek convert and later let Paul and Silas use her home as a base for the spread of Christianity throughout the western world.

But it all started with an ex-madman, who, instead of being numbered among Jesus' disciples, returned to his town and told everyone "how much the Lord had done" for him.

> Father, I pray that those of us who have been on the receiving end of Your miracles will have the boldness to tell somebody, even if we never get any credit or glory. For the Kingdom's sake. Amen.

FOUR

HEALED BY THE FAITH OF FRIENDS

Persons Are More Important Than Property

"They went up on the roof and lowered him on his mat through the tiles into the middle of the crowd, right in front of Jesus."

MATTHEW 9:1-8
(Also Mark 2:3-12; Luke 5:18-26)

Jesus stepped into a boat, crossed over and came to His own town. Some men brought to Him a paralytic, lying on a mat. When Jesus saw their faith, He said to the paralytic, "Take heart, son; your sins are forgiven."

At this, some of the teachers of the law said to themselves, "This fellow is blaspheming!"

Knowing their thoughts, Jesus said, "Why do you entertain evil thoughts in your hearts? Which is easier: to say, 'Your sins are forgiven,' or to say, 'Get up and walk'? But so that you may know that the Son of Man has authority on earth to forgive sins . . ." Then He said to the paralytic, "Get up, take your mat and go home." And the man got up and went home. When the crowd saw this, they were filled with awe;

and they praised God, who had given such authority
to men.

Shortly after Jesus began His public ministry He moved
to the little seacoast town of Capernaum, on the north
coast of the Sea of Galilee. He had lived in Nazareth since
He was a small child, but it is difficult to minister in your
home town. Even though He had chosen the little village
of Cana, almost within a stone's throw of Nazareth, as
the site for His first miracle, things had not gone well
in Nazareth.

Immediately after His first miracle, which occurred on
a Wednesday afternoon, He went up to Capernaum,
teaching and performing miracles. Friday afternoon a week
later, He returned to Nazareth. Saturday morning, as was
His custom since He was a boy, He went to the little
synagogue, where it was His time to read. One of the
rabbis handed Him the scroll of the prophet Isaiah.
Unrolling it, He found the place He wanted to read:

> The Spirit of the Lord is on me,
> because he has anointed me
> to preach good news to the poor.
> He has sent me to proclaim freedom for the prisoners
> And recovery of sight for the blind,
> to release the oppressed,
> to proclaim the year of the Lord's favor.

He then sat down. There was an uncomfortable silence,
accompanied by the shuffling of feet and clearing of
throats. No one said anything. Then He stood back up.
Everyone knew the Scripture He had just read pertained
to the coming Messiah. "Today this Scripture is fulfilled
in your hearing," He said.

"Aw, come on," they jested. "We know who You are.

You're Joseph's son. How can You say You're the Son of God?"

"I tell you the truth," Jesus answered, "no prophet is accepted in his home town. . . ."

The people in the synagogue were furious. They felt they had not only been rebuked by this young upstart carpenter, they felt He was blaspheming God—a crime punishable by death. Roaring in anger, the mob rushed Him. Jesus fled, running before them. They chased Him to the edge of a cliff, intending to throw Him over the side. Then another miracle took place: as the mob rushed toward Him, He turned and calmly walked through them, as though He had become invisible. He didn't stop walking, but kept going, east to the Sea of Galilee and on to Capernaum. He never returned to Nazareth to live. Since then the little town has never known the power and blessing of God. Even today, in modern Israel, it is one of the few towns with a Communist mayor.

However, Jesus' ministry in Capernaum flourished. The people were receptive—open not only to His miracles, but to His teaching. Of course there was opposition, as there was all over Israel, from the religious leaders who were threatened by His ministry. It's so much safer to talk about a coming Messiah than it is to welcome *the* Messiah. Thus, every place Jesus went, even in Capernaum, He was met by two kinds of people—those who were eager to know more about God, and those who felt they knew all there was to know about God.

Jesus stepped into a boat, crossed over and came to His own town.

It was the following summer, about a year after He had left Nazareth, that Jesus arrived early one morning on one of the fishing boats which still pull into the nearby wharves after fishing all night on the lake. The evening before He had been through a terrifying experience on the eastern shore of the lake when accosted by a wild man, full of demons, who had tried to kill Him. Instead, Jesus had sent the demons into a nearby herd of pigs which had rushed into the sea and drowned. No doubt His Jewish disciples were still chuckling over that, seeing it as poetic justice: no Jewish farmer had the right to raise swine, which was forbidden food under the kosher laws.

Arriving in Capernaum, Jesus went immediately to the house of a friend. Within minutes word had spread He was there. People began to gather.

Life in the Galilee region was public. Each morning the housekeeper would open her front door as an invitation for friends and neighbors to stop by. The door was shut only at night. The open door meant "Come in." Most of the houses were small, and even though there might be a front courtyard, there was seldom an entrance hall. Visitors, then, came in right off the street.

In no time a crowd had filled the little house, jamming the courtyard as well. The people, unlike those in Nazareth, were eager to hear what Jesus had to say—and to see the miracles which by now occurred everyplace He went.

In telling the story Mark says, "He preached the word to them." What is the word? It was not what we now think of as "the word." When we use that phrase today we mean the written word—the Bible. But there was no Bible in Jesus' day, only the books of the law, the books of the prophets, and the Psalms—and these were in huge scrolls which were confined to the synagogue. The teaching or preaching of "the word," then, meant that Jesus was speaking whatever the Holy Spirit told Him to speak. The Greek word is *rhema*—the spoken word, the "now" word, the word of the Holy Spirit. Jesus loved the Torah, but

He used it only to confirm what God was saying today—
not to talk (as the scribes did) of what God said yesterday.

Some men brought to Him a paralytic, lying on a mat.

Both Mark and Luke give greater detail than Matthew
does here. They tell us that the four men arrived carrying
the stretcher, or mat, on which the paralyzed man was
lying. There was no way to get him into the house, or
even into the courtyard for that matter. So they took
another approach.

The typical roof on a Galilean house was almost flat,
with just enough slant for the water to drain off. Since
the houses were open and there was little privacy, the
roof was regularly used as a place of rest and quiet.
Many of the houses had an outside stairway leading to
the roof, which might be surrounded by a low parapet.
On other houses the roof was reached by a ladder.

The roof itself consisted of flat beams laid across the
walls of the house, perhaps three feet apart. Brushwood
and palm fronds were laid across the beams. Mud, clay,
and sod were then put on the brushwood. When this
mixture dried, it was strong enough to support the weight
of several men. Occasionally, when it rained, the dirt would
sprout grass, meaning the owner of the house would have
to tether his goat on the roof to cut the grass. Despite
its strength, however, it would have been a relatively simple
matter to break through the roof into the house—although
to do so would have made a big mess down below.

The four men, realizing they would never be able to
get their friend into the house through the door, lifted
him to the roof. Digging out the filling between the beams,
they lowered the man, accompanied by a rain of dirt and
debris, directly in front of where Jesus was standing.
Question: who paid for the roof? Probably the same

person who reimbursed the pig farmer the night before. It was expensive to be around Jesus. The pig farmer just had to tighten his belt and absorb his losses. There was no government agriculture department to provide disaster aid or a low-interest emergency loan. The same was true of the homeowner where Jesus was teaching. It could cost you something to invite Jesus into your house.

This is true today. When Jesus comes into a person's life, it often upsets the routine. One man said he was required by God to loan his expensive car to a family who needed transportation. Another said God asked him to open his home to strangers, who often abused his house and sometimes stole from him. One family took in foster children who were unwanted by their parents, and inherited huge problems by doing so. Building God's Kingdom costs.

But the destruction of the roof didn't seem to bother Jesus. He smiled at these men who weren't stopped by barriers, who kept trying until they were able to get their paralyzed friend into Jesus' presence. Such perseverance. Such faith.

I wonder what it was like to be part of the audience that day. The people are comfortable, enjoying a splendid sermon, when suddenly dirt and sticks begin falling on their heads. Suddenly, the roof opens up and they see four faces peering down through the hole. Moments later the four are lowering a fifth man through the hole, just as pallbearers would lower a casket into a grave.

> When Jesus saw their faith, He said to the paralytic, "Son, your sins are forgiven."

When Jesus saw their faith. Whose faith? The faith of the crowd? Don't discount it. I remember attending some of those miracle services in the huge Shrine Auditorium in Los Angeles conducted by the late Kathryn Kuhlman. I interviewed people who had been healed in those meetings. Some of them had no faith whatsoever. Some didn't even believe in God, much less in His Son, Jesus. Yet they were healed. There were all kinds of explanations. Most of them made sense, but the one I felt most comfortable with had to do with the faith of the crowd. The people came to those services believing. Many had been to previous services and had seen the miracles. They had told others about it. A tremendous amount of faith was generated. It was more than the expectancy factor— it was faith. They came believing God would meet them. Sometimes, as I approached the meeting hall, I could sense the faith several blocks away. I talked to one man who had been healed in his car in the parking lot before he could even get into the building.

There was that same kind of faith factor in the crowd that jammed the house in Capernaum. They were excited. They came expecting something to happen.

I've seen that in my own church building on a number of occasions. I know of folks who arrived for a regular Sunday morning worship service believing they were going to be healed that morning—and they were. I talked to an older man who was visiting our church for the first time. He said the moment he came through the doors of the auditorium he was healed of chronic arthritis which had been so painful he could hardly walk.

"How can this be?" he asked me after the service. "I'm not even sure I believe in God."

"Who do you think healed you?"

"It must have been God," he said. "But I never even prayed."

"God is here in the presence of His people," I told him. "It's not that God fills the room; rather, God fills our hearts. When the people of God gather, something happens."

It's the faith of the crowd.

Yet as important as that is, when Jesus spoke of "their faith," He was not referring to the crowd; He was obviously thinking about the man's four friends. It takes an awful lot of faith to break through the roof of somebody's house and lower a paralytic through the hole into a church service going on down below.

Such faith is still present in the world, still bringing healing. Many can testify to the faith of their parents. Carlyle once said that still, across the years, there came his mother's voice to him, "Trust in God and do right." The great poet and essayist said his mother's faith strengthened him throughout his life. When Augustine was living a wild and immoral life, his devout mother came to ask help from a Christian bishop. "It is impossible," the bishop told her, "that the child of so many prayers and tears should perish." Augustine says it was the faith of his godly mother, like the faith of those four friends, which brought him to Jesus.

Sensing the faith in the room, Jesus looked at the paralytic and said simply, "Your sins are forgiven."

Why forgive his sins? What the man needed was a physical overhaul. He was paralyzed. He couldn't walk. It seems that's what most preachers do: they overlook the obvious—the things they can't (or won't) do anything about—and focus on the spiritual. But remember, the Jews equated all physical suffering with sin. They believed that if a man was suffering, it was the result of sin. That was the argument Job's "friend," Eliphaz, used. "Who, being innocent, has ever perished? Where were the upright ever destroyed?" he asked Job (Job 4:7). He was saying what the old rabbis said much later, "There is no sick man healed of his sickness until all his sins have been forgiven him." That's the reason Jesus began by saying, "Your sins are forgiven."

To the Jews a sick man was a man with whom God was angry.

I have a friend who is continually sick. When I ask him why, he always gives the same answer. "God is punishing me for my sin," he says. His "sin" was that he went to the wrong school 30 years before. He said he knew God wanted him to go to a Christian school in Chicago; instead, he went to a Christian school in North Carolina. Ever since, he believes, God has made him sick. His concept of God is that of a policeman, or even worse, a bully.

Jesus came to reveal a different God. He said God was a loving Heavenly Father. Notice, Jesus did not require anything of the paralytic. He didn't tell him to first confess his sins. He didn't lead him through the "sinner's prayer." He simply looked at him and absolved him of all his sins.

Now we can see why it was imperative for Jesus to forgive the man's sins as a preamble to the miracle about to follow. The man had been raised a Jew. As such, he had been taught by the rabbis that his sickness, his paralysis, was the result of some sin he had committed. To have healed him without forgiving his sins would have been more than the man could have taken. But once the sin factor was out of the way, he could accept his healing.

"Son," Jesus said to him tenderly, "God is not angry with you. It's okay." To say your sins are forgiven is to say God is not angry. Jesus was doing what He always did—revealing the Father.

Mark, in his account of this story, mentions that there were some scribes and Pharisees in the room. They sat there, thinking to themselves, "Why does this fellow talk like that? He's blaspheming! Who can forgive sins but God alone?" (Mark 2:6,7).

Jesus knew what they were thinking. I can see Him,

turning to His disciples and grinning, as if to say, "Let's see if they can wiggle out of this one." Then He replied, even before the scribes had a chance to argue.

> *Which is easier: to say to the paralytic, "Your sins are forgiven," or to say, "Get up, take your mat and walk"?*

I imagine He had to work hard to suppress His laughter. The Jews said you can't be healed unless your sins are forgiven. So, for their sake, it was paramount that He say to this man, "Your sins are forgiven." But they also said that only God could forgive sin. Therefore, the moment Jesus forgave the man's sin, He set Himself up as God. Now the scribes were trapped. Now they had to make a decision: is He God, or is He not? They were going to say no, of course, He is not God. So Jesus came right back and said, "Okay, which is easier to say: your sins are forgiven, or, get up and walk?"

The Jews didn't have the power to say either. The scribes knew they didn't have the power to heal, and they were afraid to say they could forgive sin—that would be blasphemy.

The Jews had a complicated system by which sin was forgiven. On Yom Kippur, the Day of Atonement, the high priest entered the inner sanctum of the Temple, the Holy of Holies. Only the high priest could enter the Holy of Holies, and then only on the Day of Atonement. He would then sprinkle blood on the Ark of the Covenant as an atonement for the sins of the people. On the basis of that, sins were forgiven.

Therefore, when Jesus dared to forgive sin in another manner, a manner which seemed not only flippant, but irreligious, they called Him a blasphemer. Jesus was not following procedure. Instead of following the religious rules, He acted as God directed.

Suddenly the atmosphere in the house turned hostile. The faith factor was gone. The room was filled with doubt and conflict.

Jesus knew just how deep He had dug, for there was even more at stake: vested interest. It was built into the religious system that in order to obtain forgiveness, every Jew had to make at least one pilgrimage a year to the Temple in Jerusalem. For sin to be forgiven, the law called for blood sacrifice. That meant each Jew had to have blood shed on his behalf.

In the Court of the Gentiles, despite the sanctity of the Temple area, there was a flourishing trade in sacrificial animals. There were shops where pilgrims who had come up to Jerusalem to worship in the Temple could buy oxen, sheep, and doves which could then be offered up in the appropriate sacrifices. It was naturally more convenient for the pilgrims to be able to buy within the precincts an animal already certified as suitable, than to have to bring an animal with him which would also then have to undergo an official inspection—and perhaps be declared unworthy.

There were also tables where money-changers changed money for the payment of the animal Temple tax. Most of the circulating currency in Judea was Roman money, and because such coins bore a portrait of the emperor, which the Jews considered unacceptable for sacred offerings based on the second commandment, it had to be changed into a special coinage which was the only legal fare for Temple dues. Of course the money-changer made a profit on each exchange.

This profitable trade, which was supported by the powerful high-priestly family of Annas and Caiaphas, was being held in the Temple precincts in the Court of the Gentiles for the first time. Customarily, pilgrims had bought ritually pure objects of sacrifice for the Temple offerings at the four markets on the Mount of Olives opposite (which were considered a part of the Temple precincts for ritual purposes). These markets, however, were under the jurisdiction of the Sanhedrin and not of the high priest. So Caiaphas, the high priest, introduced a sale of animals in the Temple itself in competition with the traditional markets on the Mount of Olives. Caiaphas had long been struggling for power and authority with the Sanhedrin; this move, which coincided with the beginning of Jesus' ministry in Galilee, gave him the chance of scoring an important financial gain over his enemies.

It was the people, of course, who suffered from the greed of the leaders. They were required by law to purchase the necessary ingredients for forgiveness—or remain in their sins (and their sickness).

Therefore, when Jesus brashly stepped forward and said, "Your sins are forgiven" without requiring that the man go buy a pigeon from a pigeon vendor, He was threatening not only the theological system, but the entire economic system of the religious structure.

If you want to get a man angry in a hurry, just take money out of his pocket that he thought he was going to get. Even the most godly people get bent out of shape if you threaten their financial structure, do something to cause their donations to dry up, or mess with their "partners"—the ones who support their ministry by sending them money each month.

The scribes and Pharisees, seeing just how dangerous this "free forgiveness" could be, were burning with anger. Not only could they not say "rise and walk," they were about to lose their source of income.

At this point Jesus was ready to pull out all the stops. Up to now He had been having a good time, almost playing with these religious sticks-in-the-mud. But now it was time to get serious. Looking over at His disciples, He winked. Then He turned, looked down at the paralytic, and said, "Get up, take your mat, and go home."

Mark says the man "got up, took his mat and walked out in full view of them all" (Mark 2:12). You can almost hear Jesus' disciples, and the others in the room who had been enjoying the one-way repartee, burst into applause and shouting. That's the way it ought to happen! Just take authority, and healing is yours. In fact, Matthew concludes the story by saying, "When the crowd saw this, they were filled with awe; and they praised God, who had given such authority to men" (Matthew 9:8).

Is such healing for today? Dr. Paul Tournier in *A Doctor's Case Book* tells a fascinating story which answers that question with a resounding "yes!"

"There was, for example, the girl whom one of my friends had been treating several months for anemia, without much success. As a last resort, my colleague decided to send her to the medical officer of the district in which she worked, in order to get his permission to send her to a mountain sanitarium. A week later the patient brought word back from the medical officer. He appeared to be a good fellow, and he had granted the permit, 'But,' he added, 'analyzing the blood, however, I do not arrive at anything like the figures you quote.'

"My friend, somewhat put out, at once took a fresh sample of the blood and rushed it to a laboratory. Sure enough, the blood count had suddenly changed. 'If I had not been the kind of person who keeps careful laboratory routines,' my friend's story goes on, 'if I had not previously checked my figures at each of my patient's visits, I would have thought I had made a mistake.' So

> he turned to the patient and asked her, 'Has
> anything else out of the ordinary happened in your
> life since your last visit?' 'Yes, something has
> happened,' she replied. 'I have suddenly been able
> to forgive someone against whom I bore a nasty
> grudge, and all at once I felt I could at last say
> yes to life.' "

On the basis of forgiving someone she had a grudge against, and saying yes to life, the blood count had changed. The anemia was gone, and the medical doctors recognized it in the laboratory.

A miracle. But a miracle with reason. All miracles have God's reason behind them. In this case, Jesus said to the man, "Your sins are forgiven," and when He said it, something sparked in this man. "God is not angry at me. God loves me! There is hope for my life." Then Jesus said, "Now take up your bed and walk," and suddenly strength went into his body and his back and his legs. But the real miracle happened in his spirit, before it happened in his flesh. It happened for the sake of his spirit, rather than just for the sake of the flesh.

"Why do you entertain evil thoughts in your heart?"

Jesus had a harsh word for the nay-sayers, those negative ones, who had in their hearts a lack of faith. He calls their lack of faith evil—a term He uses only rarely. The scribes and Pharisees were constantly accusing Jesus of blasphemy. But they had everything backwards. Lack of faith is the greatest blasphemy. Not to believe is the heart of all evil. To deliberately say "God can't heal, God can't deliver from evil spirits, God can't change circumstances"— is the foundation for all blasphemy.

Perhaps we need to once again ask the question: Why

are miracles needed? If we walk as spiritual people, then why miracles? Why don't we walk in health all the time? Why don't we walk in godly protection all the time? Are miracles only for those who are out there living in horrible sin?

No. Miracles are needed because we are sinful people. We live in a sinful world. We are part of a sinful system. We are part of the natural system which God has set in order, which has been polluted by man as he has run it. Even though I believe God would have us walk as Adam and Eve, in perfect harmony with nature, we don't do it. Because of the evil spirits, because of the Evil One, and because all of us have sinned and come short of the glory of God—we need miracles.

The only way we can exist on this earth abundantly is to walk miracle lives. That's the reason we, as God's people, should expect a miracle every day. We should be living with that, and when we walk into a situation where circumstances say, "The world says this," we should shout, "But God says that—and I'm going to go with God."

Father, I thank You for overriding the system with Your System of Miracles. I thank You that we, as Your people, have the ability to live with signs and wonders following after us. I pray, O God, hasten the day—in fact, make it now—when we are not just talking about miracles, but we will actually demonstrate them in our own lives, as we listen to You on a moment-by-moment basis. For Jesus' sake and in His power. Amen.

FIVE

HEALING THROUGH THE SPOKEN WORD
Jesus Heals a Paralyzed Man

"Get up! Pick up your mat and walk."

JOHN 5:1-15

Some time later, Jesus went up to Jerusalem for a feast of the Jews. Now there is in Jerusalem near the Sheep Gate a pool, which in Aramaic is called Bethesda and which is surrounded by five covered colonnades. Here a great number of disabled people used to lie— the blind, the lame, the paralyzed. One who was there had been an invalid for 38 years. When Jesus saw him lying there and learned that he had been in this condition for a long time, He asked him, "Do you want to get well?"

"Sir," the invalid replied, "I have no one to help me into the pool when the water is stirred. While I am trying to get in, someone else goes down ahead of me."

Then Jesus said to him, "Get up! Pick up your mat and walk." At once the man was cured; he picked up his mat and walked.

The day on which this took place was a Sabbath, and so the Jews said to the man who had been healed, "It is the Sabbath; the law forbids you to carry your mat."

But he replied, "The man who made me well said to me, 'Pick up your mat and walk.' " So they asked him, "Who is this fellow who told you to pick it up and walk?"

The man who was healed had no idea who it was, for Jesus had slipped away into the crowd that was there.

Later Jesus found him at the temple and said to him, "See, you are well again. Stop sinning or something worse may happen to you." The man went away and told the Jews that it was Jesus who had made him well.

In the days of Christ there was in the literature of the Jewish nation a group of writings called "the Scriptures"— now called the Old Testament. These were the books of history, books of poetry, and the writings of the prophets. All were considered inspired, although the historical books—known as the Torah—were considered the most important.

Early in the fourth century, the Roman emperor, Constantine, who had become a Christian, wrote a letter to Eusebius, bishop of Caesarea, asking him to compile those writings of the early church which he felt to be inspired. Constantine asked him to employ skillful copyists to put together fifty Bibles to be used in the churches of Constantinople.

Eusebius was forced to select from a number of writings. Many of these were considered spurious. These included "The Acts of Paul," "Shepherd of Hermas," "Apocalypse of Peter," and the "Epistle of Barnabas." Others were declared forgeries of heretics, such as the "Gospel of Peter," the "Gospel of Thomas," and the "Acts of Andrew." What books constituted the New Testament of Eusebius? Exactly the same books that now constitute the New Testament.

Later the Council of Carthage, meeting in A.D. 397, gave formal ratification to the 27 books of the New Testament.

The original manuscripts of all the New Testament books, as far as is known, have been lost. The writing material in common use was papyrus, made of thin slices of the stalk of a water plant. Two slices, one vertical, the other horizontal, were pressed together and polished. Ink was made from charcoal, gum, and water—written with a quill or sharpened feather. These sheets were fastened side to side to form rolls which could be 30 feet long and 10 inches high.

By the fourth century new materials were available. Eusebius had his copiers write on vellum, a parchment made from skins.

The chapters and verses were not marked in the original text. The first place markings were added by Cardinal Caro in A.D. 1236 and later perfected by Robert Stephens in A.D. 1551. However, as serious students of the Bible know, many of these chapter and verse divisions are misplaced; still, they do make the actual Scriptures much easier to locate and remember.

Most Bible scholars agree that in the ordering of the materials in the book of John, the sixth chapter should precede the fifth chapter. In fact, many of the events listed in the four biographies of Jesus (Matthew, Mark, Luke, and John) seem to be in non-chronological order, especially when you compare the Gospels with each other. That has nothing to do with the inspiration of the Scriptures. It is simply an indication that in the various copyings across the centuries, the writing of what is now John 5 got placed before what is now John 6.

One of the reasons most Bible scholars feel the sixth chapter should come first has to do with the feasts that are mentioned in those chapters. There were three Jewish feasts of obligation. Every adult male Jew who lived within

20 miles of Jerusalem was legally bound to attend these three feasts. People came from much farther away than 20 miles, but the obligation was for those within 20 miles by the law of the Sanhedrin. Those three feasts were the feast of Passover, the feast of Pentecost, and the feast of Tabernacles.

John always shows us Jesus attending the great feasts. These were celebration times when the whole nation would enter into an entire week of feasting and celebration. Those feast are still conducted, to some degree, in Israel. The feast of Pentecost does not have nearly as strong an emphasis as the time of Passover and the time of Tabernacles. But if you are in Israel during the time of these great feasts, you will find the people celebrating.

The sixth chapter of John begins with the biographer writing: "The Jewish Passover feast was near" (John 6:4). The Passover was in mid-April, and Pentecoast was seven weeks later. So Pentecost would be the next official feast in the Jewish calendar. Thus, since the feast in John 6 was Passover, the feast mentioned in John 5 was undoubtedly Pentecost. Following this, Jesus returned to the Galilee region where He remained for a few months. Then He returned to Jerusalem. The seventh chapter of John opens with Jesus attending still another feast, the feast of Tabernacles, which was always held in early fall at the time of harvest. Thus the correct order, from a chronological standpoint, would read John 6 (Passover), 5 (Pentecost), 7 (Tabernacles).

Jesus did not disregard the obligations which Jewish worship laid on the people. It was not a duty but a delight to worship with His own people. Across the years the Christian church has allowed to go slack the various Jewish feasts, fasts, and other obligations—much to our detriment. The church needs to return to the celebration of these feasts and fasts—at least the ones God calls "everlasting."

The church, composed now primarily of gentile believers—grafted into Jewish roots—should, not by obligation, but by desire (as Jesus did) observe the biblical ceremonies. This includes our observance of the Sabbath—certainly not with legalistic fervor, but with respect toward God who ordained it. Jesus, of course, never let the Sabbath get in the way of doing God's will, but He had a deep respect for the law which said a man should rest and honor God on the seventh day of the week.

> Some time later, Jesus went up to Jerusalem for a feast of the Jews.

Jesus was apparently alone when He arrived in Jerusalem to attend the feast of Pentecost. Despite the common conception, Jesus was not surrounded by people all the time. There were important times in His life when He was alone. Having celebrated Passover in the Galilee region, He then left His disciples behind to tend to their fishing on the lake and headed south through the Jordan Valley. It was a long walk from His home in Capernaum to Jerusalem—a distance of about 110 miles. It was late spring, and temperatures in the desert regions in the Jordan Valley would have already been soaring to 100 degrees F. The walk from Jericho, near the Dead Sea, to Jerusalem—a distance of almost 30 miles—is one of the steepest ascents in the world, through one of the most foreboding sections of the world—the Judean wilderness. Yet Jesus made this trip several times in His three years of ministry, growing stronger each time.

> Now there is in Jerusalem near the Sheep Gate a pool, which in Aramaic is called Bethesda and which is surrounded by five covered colonnades. Here a great number of disabled people used to lie—the blind, the

*lame, the paralyzed—[and they waited for the moving
of the waters. From time to time an angel of the Lord
would come down and stir up the waters. The first one
into the pool after each such disturbance would be cured
of whatever disease he had.]*

Arriving in Jerusalem, He went straight to a favorite
place of rest and refreshment, the Pool of Bethesda near
the Sheep Gate of the city wall. The name Bethesda means,
literally, "house of outpouring," or "house of mercy." The
name was significant, not simply because this was a
delightful resting place for residents and travelers alike,
but because of the medicinal qualities of the waters which
may have originated with a hot sulphur spring bubbling
out of the ground. Actually, there were two pools—an upper
pool where the hot water bubbled in from underground,
and a much deeper, adjoining pool where people could
actually dive in and swim. The name Bethesda designated
either the pool itself or the huge, ornate building which
surrounded the pools with five covered colonnades or tiled
porches.

Not only would weary travelers gather under the roofs
of these porches, but a large number of sick people came
here to bathe in the waters. The day Jesus arrived He
found the place crowded with a number of disabled
people—the blind, the lame, the paralyzed. The original
text of John's biography does not include the latter part
of verse 3 and verse 4, which I have marked in brackets.
This seems to have been added later as an explanation
of why these sick people came to the pool. It was a common
saying that the "moving of the waters" was caused by an
angel who came down and stirred them. Actually there
was, beneath the pool, a hot, subterranean stream which
every now and then bubbled up and disturbed the waters
of the upper pool. When this happened, the people would

rush for the water to take advantage of its medicinal value.

Many people, including a large number in the medical community, believe there are medicinal qualities in the water that geysers from the earth. In fact, a large number of healing centers have grown up around various "hot springs." There is a healing center at Hot Springs, Arkansas. President Franklin Roosevelt, confined to a wheelchair as a victim of polio, had a home at Warm Springs, Georgia, where he bathed in the hot water which came from the earth. Doctors are unsure exactly what causes the healing—whether it is the warm water, the minerals in the water, or the bubbling effect. I know that on several occasions, during my long treks through the Sinai Peninsula researching the "wilderness experience" of the children of Israel, I have bathed at such a spring on the Gulf of Suez on the west coast of the Sinai, at a place called E-tor. Here hot sulphur water bubbles into a bricked-in enclosure, and weary desert travelers, their bones aching from fatigue and skin parched from the hot, dry wind, find instant refreshment as they soak in the hot springs. Although I doubt such bathings, even on a daily basis, would cure a congenital deformity, I can certainly see how it would be good for diseases such as arthritis. Even more I can understand why the sick in ancient times, lacking today's wonderful medical expertise, would flock to such a place as the Pool of Bethesda.

One who was there had been an invalid for 38 years. When Jesus saw him lying there and learned that he had been in this condition for a long time, He asked him, "Do you want to get well?"

It was a natural question. If a person does not want to get well, there is no healing. Even the best physician cannot bring healing if the person refuses it. The first step in seeing a miracle is the desire to see a miracle. That's not to say God does not perform miracles where there is no desire, no faith, no willingness to see a miracle. There are countless instances on record where God performed miracles among people who didn't even know God existed, much less was a God of miracles.

However, God is always looking at our hearts. If our heart—that is, the real us—does not want a miracle, chances are good we'll never receive one.

However, this man had been wanting to be healed for 38 years. That was the length of time he had been sick. John does not say exactly what was wrong with him. The King James Version said the man was impotent. A better translation is powerless, unable to move, perhaps even paralyzed. His family or friends probably brought him to the pool each morning, arranged his mat under the porches so he would not be baked in the sun, and left him there to beg. During the dry months of the year the geyser beneath the pool may have bubbled only infrequently. Sometimes the man would wait there for weeks at a time with the water simply lying stale and tepid. During the rainy season, when the water level in the ground was higher, the geyser might bubble daily. Yet the selfish people around the old begger never helped him. Year after year he had lain there, his hand extended for a few coins, hoping in his heart someone would come along and lower him into the pool just as the bubbling began . . . but it never happened.

Now he had grown old. It was no longer his parents who brought him to the pool, for they had long since died. Now it was his nephews who, day by day, lifted his frail body and brought him to his familiar place under the colonnades—his home away from home. But he had long ago given up any hope of being healed. So year after year, he lay under the colonnades at the Pool of

Bethesda. He lived in the hospital, a permanent resident of the clinic. He had long since discovered no one cared enough to help him into the water. He was resigned, like the hundreds of other beggars in the city, to living a miserable life of hopelessness.

Then one morning this strong young man appeared and asked if he wanted to be healed.

What must have gone through the old panhandler's dull mind? Was this fellow just playing with him, as a cat toys with a mouse or lizard? Was he some kind of government official, preparing to tell him he could no longer lie under the colonnades? Or could it be the young man really cared? Was it possible this stranger might lift him and put him in the waters of the pool—waters the old man believed were more than medicinal, they were magic? "Hey, old man," one of the other nearby beggars hooted, "don't get your hopes up. Not today. Today's shabbot, the sabbath. Even if He wanted to help you, He can't. The law says you can't pick up a burden on the sabbath—and if you're anything, you're a burden. Har! Har!"

"Do you want to be well?" Jesus had asked.

Sickness has its benefits. People pay more attention to you when you are sick than when you are well. You are able to shirk responsibility if you are sick; after all, everyone knows you can't function, so they don't expect as much from you. Most people are tender and gentle when they are around sick people. Even the government favors the sick, providing financial assistance if you are disabled.

Several years ago I was speaking in a small church in Columbia, South Carolina, on the miracle power of Jesus. After one of the morning services two young men came forward, accompanying a beautiful blind girl in her late twenties. They told me that as a young teenager she had been injured in an accident. Over the next two years she had lost her sight. Now she was only able to distinguish light from dark. Did I believe, they wanted to know, that God could restore her sight?

I looked at her and asked the same question Jesus asked. "Do you want to see?"

She immediately said, "Yes, of course." But I sensed something in her voice, and asked her again.

"Are you telling me the truth?"

She exploded. "Why don't you all leave me alone!"

Turning, she started back down the aisle of the church, feeling her way along the ends of the pews, her white cane sweeping in front of her.

I left her friends and followed her to the door. Stopping her, gently, I said, "I understand."

She broke into tears. "It's not that I don't believe God can heal me," she said. "I know He can. I've known it for a long time. But I'm happy the way I am. People care for me. No one's ever done that before. I have a good income from the government . . ."

"And you're afraid of losing all that," I interrupted.

Her tears continued. "What's wrong with being blind?" she blurted. "Can't I still be useful to God?"

"Years ago," I told her, "another talented man, a great poet, asked the same question of God when he went blind at the peak of his career. In his sonnet on his blindness, John Milton asked: 'Doth God exact day-labor, light denied?' "

"Does He?" she asked, her sightless eyes staring at me. I answered her from Milton.

"Who best
Bear his mild yoke, they serve him best; his state
Is kingly; thousands at his bidding speed,
And post o'er land and ocean without rest;
They also serve who only stand and wait."

"Does that mean God will still love me if I don't ask Him to heal me?"

"Of course," I answered, holding her as she wept against my chest. "But it means you will miss the bigger adventure."

She smiled. "You asked if I want to see, and I lied. Deep in my heart I want to be just the way I am."

"Then you shall remain that way," I answered. "And God will love you and use you in your blindness."

She turned and left, tapping her way down the sidewalk with her white cane. I watched her go, sad, for I knew God would have given her whatever she asked—but she was afraid of the change.

Life is designed by God to be fun and an adventure. God has placed in each of us a part of His own nature. As the creative part of God is in us, meaning we can never be totally fulfilled in life unless we are creating, so the adventurous part of God is in us also. We can never be really fulfilled unless we are venturing out—that is, exercising our faith (which is adventure in action). They look at circumstances and call them calamities rather than challenges. They do not understand that there are no calamities in the life of the believer, only challenges. This is just as true whether life serves you blindness or a prison cell—all remain great adventures, challenges, opportunities to serve God and exercise great faith in the spirit of adventure.

Does that mean every blind person should pray for sight? That every prisoner should believe God will throw open his cell door as He did for Peter and later for Paul and Silas? No, but it does mean that when circumstances visit us with blindness, incarceration, or paralysis we must answer the question: Do I want to be healed, do I want to see, do I want to be set free? If you do, there are certain things God will require of you—and many are not willing to pay that price.

I remember old Mrs. Jessie Stewart, a member of the founding family of the little east coast Florida town where

I lived. She was a great adventurer. At the age of 82 she helped start a new church—a church which has now grown to be the largest church in the city. But three years after she and a small group of her friends began that ministry, she fell in her home (she was living alone) and broke her back. Her granddaughter felt it was best to have her confined to a convalescent home.

It was a sad experience. As a youth this beautiful girl, along with her young husband, had ridden her horse down the east coast of Florida when it was nothing more than a mosquito-infested swamp. Battling alligators and rattlesnakes and fighting off the wild bears, they built their house with their own hands. Across the years this adventurous woman had out-lived not only her two husbands, but her children and nearly all of the other people who had moved to Florida in those years at the turn of the century. Now, like a great she-tiger which had once claimed the entire jungle as her home, she was forced to spend her final days on earth in the cage of a convalescent home.

Yet when I went to visit her she said, "Isn't this wonderful?"

I looked around. Wonderful? Here was this great, adventurous spirit, not only confined in a body that no longer worked, but strapped into a bed in a tiny room in a building where the smell of urine and disinfectant was so strong it made my eyes water. Standing beside her bed I could hear the other patients moaning and groaning up and down the halls. Some, like Jessie Stewart, were confined to their beds. Others were sitting in wheelchairs in the halls, staring at the walls. To me it was the most depressing place in the world—and she called it "wonderful."

"I never know from day to day what marvelous things God has in store down here," she smiled. "Why just last

night I met an old woman who had not had a visit from
anyone since she's been here—three years. She's in a
wheelchair and the nurse was pushing her by the door
when God told me to invite her in. She's coming back
tonight and we're going to study the Bible together. She
said she wants to bring some others with her. They want
me to teach them about God. Isn't that marvelous?"

Eighty-five years old, her body dying with a broken
back—but her spirit still filled with adventure.

I remember a line from Peter Pan. Peter is trapped
on a rock in the middle of a lagoon watching the tide
come in. "To die," he says, "will be an awfully big
adventure." But it was this adventurous spirit, this
willingness to risk, which gave Peter the ability to fly.

Life is designed to be an adventure. Jesus knew that,
of course, since He was the architect who was with the
Creator when life was formed. Thus, when He came to
earth and saw this wretched old man at the Pool of
Bethesda, the first question He asked was: "Is the spirit
of adventure still alive, or have you given up hope?"

The man Jesus questioned had been trapped by life's
circumstances. For 38 years he has been lying there looking
for a cure. Many adults are like that. Their entire adult
life has been spent in a doctor's office. They go to the
doctor three times a week. They are more familiar with
the doctor's office than they are with their own home.
They know where all the magazines are. Any time there
is a twitch or pain they contact their insurance company
or some government agency. They don't want to be well.
Sickness is their way of life. To change it would deprive
them of their happiness, their identity.

So many are like this man. They may not be paralyzed
in body, but their brain has stopped hoping, their heart
stopped believing. The adventurous spirit has been
crushed by life's calamities. Locked in a cell, disabled by

disease, deserted by loved ones, ostracized by society, doomed to live alone when everything in them cries out for companionship—they simply give up.

Bruce Larson tells a remarkable story about a rather gifted clergyman friend of his who confided in him one day. He said, "I woke up and saw my wife sleeping beside me, and I realized there was no way out of our hopeless relationship. For a clergyman, divorce is unthinkable. And I don't see how either of us can change. I love her, but I don't know how to live with her. Life from now on is just going to be hell."

My word! Where is his spirit of adventure? To be linked up with somebody in an inescapable situation, handcuffed to somebody we don't like or can't get along with—what bigger challenge could there be?

When pushed into that kind of situation, God would have us say: "By golly, I'm going to do something with this. By God's strength, and by God's power, even if the partner I'm handcuffed to won't make it work, I believe God can give me the strength for two. Together with God I'll make it work!"

Most are afraid to try, however. Or they've had it beaten out of them. "It's too tough. It's not worth it. She'll never change." And away they go, crushed, paralyzed. The adventurous spirit is gone.

I talked to an executive who had just returned from a conference on creative relationships sponsored by his company and run by a team of social scientists. He said, "When we arrived at the conference, I looked around the room and saw it was filled with people like me—top executives in their companies. The leader stood and said, 'I want each of you to tell who you are apart from your job or title.' Nobody in the room could answer." They didn't know who they were, apart from their job or apart from their title.

Psychologists know that if you ask a man who he is, he will invariably answer in terms of his job. "I'm an engineer." "I work for the airlines." "I'm a short-order cook at the Greasy Spoon."

But if you ask a woman you'll get all kinds of wonderful answers. They'll pull out the pictures of their children and grandchildren. They'll talk to you about their husbands, about their childhood. They'll relate all kinds of things, things that most men just don't think about.

It has been a long time since I asked anybody, "Who are you? What do you do? What is your task in life?" and had them tell me, "I'm a servant of God." Even pastors will talk about their job: "I'm the pastor of Such-and-Such Church"—relating to job and title rather than to the person behind that job.

I remember asking James Watt when I first met him several years ago "what he did." He smiled and said, "I serve the President of the United States." It was a great answer. Only later did I discover that his title was Secretary of the Interior.

Do you want to get well? The question must be asked, for the answer reveals the heart. Is the spirit of adventure and risk still present? Are you ready for the next step in life?

The man at the Pool of Bethesda answered the best he could, in the framework of his knowledge. He knew nothing of divine healing. He had no idea who Jesus was or what He had in mind. And even though, after all these years, he still yearned for healing, he only had faith to believe it would come if someone put him in the water.

So he did not give a simple "yes" answer. Instead, he gave Him an excuse as to why he was sick. He didn't say, "Oh, yes, by all means, more than anything in the world I want to be well. I yearn to leap to my feet and pick up my bed and walk. That's what I want more than anything."

Instead he answered, "Sir, You don't understand. They won't put me in the pool. I'm sick because of them."

He made an end run around the question. We hear it all the time. "My friends have let me down. My wife doesn't understand me. My mother was a neurotic. My father was an alcoholic. My older brother cheated me out of what was rightfully mine. My sister lied about me. I got beat all the time when I was a child. Someone started me on dope. The D.A. railroaded me to jail. The judge didn't give me a fair shake.

"You see, it's really not my fault that I'm this way. They've done it to me. They've shaped my life. They've made me the way I am. And here I am. My dad hit me with a bat when I was a kid, and that's the reason my back is broken. It's his fault that I'm this way. Now my friends have let me down. They won't put me in the water so I can be healed. They're all against me. Sir, You don't understand."

Jesus didn't ask for all of that. He said, "Do you want to be well?" That's all He asked. But His question stirred the slumbering excuses because Jesus touched the real man. There's something comfortable about being able to blame others for our problems. If we are not responsible for our problems, then we don't have to shoulder the responsibility ourselves.

Jesus' question touches us all. Are we willing to pay the price of change? Illness has its fringe benefits. In fact, the older this nation grows, the better off you are if you're sick. Many people never work a day in their lives because there are enough fringe benefits to keep them going. That's not to say we, personally, as a church, or through our tax dollars, should not help those who can't help themselves. Jesus' concern is for those who could help themselves—but won't. These are the ones who have discovered the government gravy train and, using their calamity, decide society owes them something. Perhaps it does, but the adventurous spirit ought to cause us to say, "I don't need society's help, I need God."

Recently I met a man who looked strong as a bull. When I shook his hand, however, he winced and gasped "Ooooh!" It was his way of telling me he was a sick man and was not available for Kingdom work. His wife worked like a dog and supported him while he stayed home and watched the soaps on television. Being sick was the best thing that ever happened to this guy.

It's not just men. Women have discovered the secret also. "Now, children, let's not upset Mother. She has another one of her migraines. So tonight we'll fix supper and do the dishes and baby her."

Sometimes having a headache is a blessing. In fact, I have discovered if I moan a little bit, and make little please-feel-sorry-for-me noises, people do all kinds of nice things for me.

Jesus' question did not deal just with illness. It dealt with wholeness. "Do you want to be made whole?" Do you want life now, in the present? Do you want the spirit of adventure restored to you?

Despite the man's seemingly poor answer, Jesus saw something in him the man didn't even see in himself. He looked deep inside of him, and He saw 38 years of being crushed by disease and pain. He didn't rebuke the man for his superstition. Rather, He took what little faith the man had—the faith if he could ever reach the water he'd be healed—and blessed that faith. The man wanted to be healed, even though he thought he never could be since he had no one to help him. So Jesus, looking deep into the man's heart, spoke the word of healing.

That's all that is ever necessary for healing—whether it is healing for a broken heart or a crippled body. All that is needed is a word from God.

There are many healing procedures found in the Bible. In James 5:14-15 we are told to call for the elders of the church, let them anoint us with oil, and we'll be healed. In John 9:6-7, Jesus spit on the ground, made mud, wiped it in the eyes of a blind man and told him to wash in the Pool of Siloam in order to see. In Matthew 8:3, Jesus reached out and touched a leper and he was healed—but in Luke 17:11-14, Jesus told ten lepers to go and show themselves to the priests and "as they went, they were cleansed." A woman in Matthew 9:20-22, touched the hem of Jesus' garment and got His attention. To her He said, "Your faith has healed you."

There seem to be as many procedures for healing as there are situations. Yet one common thread runs through every situation—the word of God is spoken.

> Then Jesus said to him, "Get up! Pick up your mat and walk." At once the man was cured; he picked up his mat and walked.

There was no fanfare, no publicity, no announcement that the healer was coming to town. The only thing present was a desperate need, a tiny speck of faith (and it was in the wrong thing), and the spoken word of God.

Later the man was grilled by the religious leaders who were, as usual, upset because their laws had been broken. (Remember, in order for a miracle to be a miracle it must supersede the laws of nature, and often the laws of man as well.)

> The Jews said to the man who had been healed, "It is the Sabbath; the law forbids you to carry your mat."

The man, puzzled about the whole thing and not sure

why everyone wasn't rejoicing that, after 38 years, he had been healed, remained true to his character. Earlier he had blamed others that he was not healed; now he blamed the healer for making him break the law.

> *The man who made me well said to me, "Pick up your mat and walk."*

That, it seems, is a back-handed way of giving God the glory and getting off the hook of personal responsibility at the same time. Fortunately, neither the man nor the Jews knew it was Jesus of Nazareth who did the healing, so there was little they could do about it. In the excitement surrounding the man's miracle, Jesus had slipped away. However, He later found the man at the Temple.

> *"See, you are well again. Stop sinning or something worse may happen to you."*

What a strange thing to say to a man you had just healed, yet it points out several critical areas. First, Jesus knew the man was a lazy deadbeat, an irresponsible manipulator, before He healed him. God never puts conditions on His grace. He heals the just and the unjust—for He loves us all. The healing did not seem to have changed the man's character. When quizzed by the Jews, he was still as irresponsible as when quizzed by Jesus. It was this "sin" Jesus was addressing when He told the man if he didn't change his way of thinking, his sickness would return.

Does this mean God would withdraw His grace? Not at all! Did it mean Jesus would take away the man's healing? Of course not. It did mean, however, that the man would make himself sick again—and this time the condition would be even worse—if he did not start giving God the glory and taking responsibility (not credit) for his healing.

"Don't allow yourself to drop back into that mentality," Jesus was saying. "Keep your sense of life and adventure flowing inside of you. Walk even when they say you can't walk. Do it even when they say it shouldn't be done since it's the Sabbath. Do the impossible. Believe the impossible. The moment you start looking at the circumstances, rather than looking at Me, you will sink beneath the waves."

The man or woman who has been delivered from alcohol or drugs knows the danger of returning to the old way of life. You know that the second encounter may be your last. The chemical process keeps going even while you are sober, and a return to drinking means you pick up as if you had been drinking all along. Therefore a man who was an alcoholic for ten years then sober for the next twenty years would immediately have the symptoms of a man who had been drunk for thirty years if he started drinking again.

Jesus says to us all: Do not focus your life on the circumstances, nor even on the visual evidence of disease or healing. Focus on Jesus and His word.

Some years ago I interviewed Dr. Clifton Harris, a medical doctor who had experienced a miracle healing. Dr. Harris, a former Southern Baptist medical missionary to China, had returned to the States during China's Communist takeover and was practicing medicine in Louisiana. His hip had been crushed in an automobile accident and the hip socket had fused with calcium. For several years he had practiced medicine from a wheelchair, but the pain had grown worse and his orthopedic surgeon had scheduled him for surgery to receive an artificial hip.

Several weeks before the surgery, friends talked him into attending a "miracle service" conducted by the late Kathryn Kuhlman, a woman minister whom God was using to perform miracles of healing. Even though he did not believe in women preachers or in divine healing, he agreed to attend the service in his wheelchair.

As the service progressed, he felt a strange heat surging through his body. Elated, he rose to his feet and walked, without pain, to the platform to testify about what was happening to him. When Miss Kuhlman prayed for him, he experienced another supernatural phenomenon—he temporarily lost consciousness and crashed backwards to the floor, landing on his injured hip. However, when his friends helped him up, they found he had suffered no injury and the pain was still gone. He returned to his town and resumed his medical practice. He no longer needed his wheelchair.

"But," he told me, "the most interesting thing happened. I went back to my orthopedic surgeon following this healing incident, and he took additional X-rays."

He pulled out some X-ray negatives and showed them to me. One was taken before his healing and the other was taken afterwards.

"They look the same to me," I confessed.

"They are the same," he said. "See all this bone calcification in the first photo. It is still there after the healing. The orthopedic surgeon looked at that and said there was no way I could walk. He said I should be in excruciating pain. But I am walking, and there is no pain."

Dr. Harris continued to walk, and practice medicine, until he died of natural causes. The pain never returned. He was able to function normally, although the structure of his hip joint remained the same.

I remember looking at him and saying, "Yes, that's just like God. He does not want you to walk by sight, but by faith. If you look at those X-rays long enough, you'll begin to believe what you see rather than what is."

"You're right," he said. "I've had them up on the wall of my office to prove what happened. But I'm going to take them down. My walk is all the proof I need."

What does all this teach us?

First of all—you have the power to bestow the word of God on somebody else. That power and authority is resident within you. You don't have to call for the experts.

Second—you have the right to receive the word of God when it comes into your life—and be healed. Circumstances may or may not change, but healing comes through God's word, not through circumstances. We are to accept it even when circumstances seem to deny it. Miracles always defy logic and human understanding.

Miracles occur to show men that the Kingdom of God is here. Present. It is a silent Kingdom operating in this universe. Without miracles there is no proof that God is any bigger than we are. We need miracles to show men that there is a God "out there" who not only created us, but who cares for us—and is still in control of all the natural laws.

The question the disciples asked when Jesus stood up in the boat and rebuked the wind and waves is still a valid question: "Who is this? Even the wind and waves obey Him" (Mark 4:41).

Even John the Baptist, that troubled prophet who had recognized Jesus as the Lamb of God when he baptized Him, doubted. John had been close to his cousin, Jesus, no doubt playing with Him as a boy. Later, the two had separated. John had withdrawn into the rugged mountains between Jerusalem and Jericho, emerging only when he was 30 years old to preach repentance and call both the common people and the leaders of the day to righteousness. It was a lonely ministry, as the ministry of the prophet always is. Many had responded to his preaching, but few had stayed with him, for he did not have a pastor's gift or personality. Harsh, abrasive, straightforward, people loved his message but doubtlessly felt uncomfortable with him. In the end he was arrested by King Herod for publicly criticizing the king's morals and lifestyle, and was thrown into prison. While in that lonely cell, he sent a pathetic message to Jesus.

"Are You the one who was to come, or should we expect someone else?" (Luke 7:19).

Perhaps John made the mistake so many of us make. He had an image of who and what the Messiah should be. He hoped it was Jesus. In fact, he had earlier believed Jesus was the Messiah. But he wanted Jesus to do things his way; and Jesus was the exact opposite of John.

John was harsh and abrasive; Jesus was gentle and kind. John was a prophet; Jesus was far more of a disciple-maker, a teacher and pastor.

John was a loner, living alone in the caves in the Judean wilderness. Jesus was gregarious. Although there were times when He withdrew into solitude, He was basically a people-person.

John was an ascetic. He lived a life of austerity as a semi-hermit, which involved much fasting and total abstinence from the "good things" of life. Jesus loved a celebration. He attended the feasts, enjoyed eating and drinking, and on one occasion even turned water into wine so the celebration could continue.

Hearing all these reports, John did not see how this man could be the Messiah. "What proof is there?" he asked.

Jesus understood His cousin's narrow view. Looking at the messengers who came from John's prison cell, Jesus said: "Go back and report to John what you have seen and heard: The blind receive sight, the lame walk, those who have leprosy are cured, the deaf hear, the dead are raised, and the good news is preached to the poor" (Luke 7:22-23).

Then, thinking about John in that terrifying prison cell, chained to a wall and awaiting a horrible execution,

Jesus grew tender. He knew, since their lifestyles were so different, how hard it was for John to think of Him, Jesus, as the Messiah. "Blessed is the man," Jesus added, "Who does not fall away on account of Me" (Luke 7:23).

His word to John was simple: Do not look at My lifestyle, look at the results. Look at the miracles. It was the miracles which proved who He was. It was the miracles which proved God was present on earth.

Yet, when some of the cynical religious leaders came to Him and said, "Teacher, we want to see a miraculous sign from You," Jesus replied, "A wicked and adulterous generation asks for a miraculous sign" (Matthew 12:38-39).

What was the difference between John and the Pharisees? John wanted to be convinced Jesus was the Messiah. He had his face toward God. The Pharisees were looking for a way to prove Jesus was not the Messiah. To them Jesus did not show miracles. Instead, He told them they needed to repent. They didn't even believe God, much less desire the appearing of the Messiah. They would not have believed even had they seen a miracle, but would have, as they did many times, complain that it was not done their way and by their formulas.

God does not give miracles on demand. Miracles are for those who need them, not those who demand them.

During the mid-twentieth century God raised up a poor illiterate man from the hills of Kentucky as one of His great miracle-workers. Although in his later years William Branham had a worldwide preaching and healing ministry, during his earlier years he earned his living as a big game hunter and game warden. He often felt, since he only had a third grade education, that he was limited with what he could do. However, looking back at his life, it is obvious his lack of formal education in this logical and humanistic world was an asset, not a liability.

Early one morning, while Branham was living alone

in the deep backwoods of the northwestern United States, he heard a scratching at the door of his little cabin. Opening the door, he looked down and saw a straggly possum, full of mange and skin disease. Perhaps she was looking for warmth from the bitter cold, or maybe she smelled Branham's breakfast and was hungry.

Branham reached for his rifle to put the creature out of her misery. Then, loaded rifle in hand, he hesitated.

"Mrs. Possum, Jesus just spoke to me. He knows you have a terrible problem. He knows I was going to shoot you to put you out of your misery. That's why I have this rifle. But you don't have to die. You don't have to live with that mange. The Lord is going to heal you so you can go home."

He tossed her some scraps of food and she left.

The next morning there was more scratching at his door. He opened it. The possum was back. This time she had a cub with her, riding on her back. The little cub, like the mother, was also covered with scabs. Once again Branham spoke words of healing—this time to the cub as well as to the mother. He gave them food and they left.

Each morning the mother possum appeared, bringing the cub with her. Day by day the mange grew better until the morning came when she did not show up. She, and her house, had been healed by the spoken word of God.

When a Roman military commander, deeply concerned about his servant who was paralyzed and in terrible pain, came to Jesus begging for help, he said: "But just say the word, and my servant will be healed" (Matthew 8:8).

"The word is near you; it is in your mouth and in your heart, that is the word of faith we are proclaiming" (Romans 10:8), Paul says.

The spoken word of faith, in the heart and mouth of a believer, brings healing. The entire creation, ever since Adam abdicated his rightful ownership and dominion of this earth, has been waiting for God's people to once again assume authority. Writing to the Romans, Paul says, "All of creation waits with eager longing for God to reveal His sons" (Romans 8:19 TEV). He goes ahead, in a passage that is brimming with deep inuendo, to say that this creation, this earth on which we live, was made to be dominated and ruled by the sons of God. Ever since Adam, there has been a deep longing in the animal and plant kingdoms, in all the world of nature—and that includes all the universe—for man to once again assume his God-given authority and responsibility as god of this world. Thus, Paul says, there has always remained the hope "that creation itself would one day be set free from its slavery to decay and would share the glorious freedom of the children of God" (Romans 8:21 TEV).

How is that to be done? By God's people—His "sons and daughters"—assuming their rightful role as people of authority. When that happens, all that will be necessary for healings and miracles will be the spoken word, coming from God out of the mouth of a believer.

Several years ago the king of Nepal, that little nation on the northern border of India where the Himalaya mountains almost touch the sky, made a decree. He commanded that all the clocks in Nepal be set ahead 10 minutes. This, he said, would give them a 10 minute start on the much larger nation of India which had always dominated them. Despite the strangeness of the edict, it was never questioned—for the edict came from the king. Instantly, every clock in Katmandu was turned forward because the king had sent his word. It took a while—many weeks, in fact—for the word to get to all the outlying tribes, many of them living in virtual isolation in the high mountain valleys. But the instant the runner came into the village and announced the king's edict, it was obeyed. Why? Because he was king.

So it is with God's people. The moment we speak God's word of authority it must be obeyed by all His subjects. We are merely His runners, His messengers—but when we speak, we speak as He speaks.

Several weeks after Jesus was crucified, Peter and John showed up at the gate of the Temple in Jerusalem. A well-known beggar, a man crippled from birth, was sitting beside the Temple gate asking for help. Peter spoke a word of faith. "In the name of Jesus Christ of Nazareth, walk" (Acts 3:6).

This put a great fear in the hearts of all the religious leaders who were sure they had gotten rid of Jesus by having Him crucified. "My God," they swore, "that man is back in town." What man? The man Jesus. But this time He had appeared in the form of Peter and John— no longer one miracle-worker, but two.

Peter explained to the astonished people what had happened. "By faith in the name of Jesus, this man whom you see and know was made strong. It is Jesus' name and the faith that comes through Him that has given this complete healing to him, as you can all see" (Acts 3:16).

How does God heal today? He will heal anyone on the basis of His mercy. But there is great evidence He prefers to heal on the basis of inheritance. God wants to use us to heal others. God wants His miracles to come through us. That way He is sure to get the glory, for everyone knows man does not have the power to heal cripples by a spoken word. When it happens, it is obvious God has inhabited that man—and the word spoken in faith is actually the word of God.

Father, I pray we not only receive a healing word from Jesus Christ, but that we be bold enough, in His name, to speak that healing word to those who have even greater needs. Amen.

Six

Sight for Blind Eyes

Miracle at the Pool of Siloam

"Whether He is a sinner or not, I don't know. One thing I do know. I was blind but now I see."

JOHN 9:1-38

As He went along, He saw a man blind from birth. His disciples asked Him, "Rabbi, who sinned, this man or his parents, that he was born blind?"

"Neither this man nor his parents sinned," said Jesus, "but this happened so that the work of God might be displayed in his life. As long as it is day, we must do the work of Him who sent Me. Night is coming, when no one can work. While I am in the world, I am the light of the world."

Having said this, He spit on the ground, made some mud with the saliva, and put it on the man's eyes. "Go," He told him, "wash in the Pool of Siloam" [this word means "sent"]. So the man went and washed, and came home seeing.

His neighbors and those who had formerly seen him begging asked, "Isn't this the same man who used to sit and beg?" Some claimed that he was.

Others said, "No, he only looks like him."

But he himself insisted, "I am the man."

"How then were your eyes opened?" they demanded.

He replied, "The man they call Jesus made some

mud and put it on my eyes. He told me to go to Siloam and wash. So I went and washed, and then I could see."

"Where is this man?" they asked him.

"I don't know," he said.

They brought to the Pharisees the man who had been blind. Now the day on which Jesus had made the mud and opened the man's eyes was a Sabbath. Therefore the Pharisees also asked him how he had received his sight. "He put mud on my eyes," the man replied, "and I washed, and now I see."

Some of the Pharisees said, "This man is not from God, for He does not keep the Sabbath."

But others asked, "How can a sinner do such miraculous signs?" So they were divided.

Finally they turned again to the blind man. "What have you to say about Him? It was your eyes He opened."

The man replied, "He is a prophet."

The Jews still did not believe that he had been blind and had received his sight until they sent for the man's parents. "Is this your son?" they asked. "Is this the one you say was born blind? How is it that now he can see?"

"We know he is our son," the parents answered, "and we know he was born blind. But how he can see now, or who opened his eyes, we don't know. Ask him. He is of age; he will speak for himself." His parents said this because they were afraid of the Jews, for already the Jews had decided that anyone who acknowledged that Jesus was the Christ would be put out of the synagogue. That was why his parents said, "He is of age; ask him."

A second time they summoned the man who had been blind. "Give glory to God," they said. "We know this man is a sinner."

He replied, "Whether He is a sinner or not, I don't know. One thing I do know. I was blind but now I see."

Then they asked him, "What did He do to you? How did He open your eyes?"

He answered, "I have told you already and you did not listen. Why do you want to hear it again? Do you want to become His disciples, too?"

Then they hurled insults at him and said, "You are this fellow's disciple! We are disciples of Moses! We know that God spoke to Moses, but as for this fellow, we don't even know where He comes from."

The man answered, "Now that is remarkable! You don't know where He comes from, yet He opened my eyes. We know that God does not listen to sinners. He listens to the godly man who does His will. Nobody has ever heard of opening the eyes of a man born blind. If this man were not from God, He could do nothing."

To this they replied, "You were steeped in sin at birth; how dare you lecture us!" And they threw him out.

Jesus heard that they had thrown him out, and when He found him, He said, "Do you believe in the Son of Man?"

"Who is He, sir?" the man asked. "Tell me so that I may believe in Him."

Jesus said, "You have now seen Him; in fact, He is the one speaking with you."

Then the man said, "Lord, I believe," and he worshiped Him.

A miracle, basically, is the intervention of a higher law over a lower law. God has, in the creation of this earth, set in motion certain physical laws that govern the universe.

There are laws of psychology and human behavior, laws of health, laws of physics, laws of engineering—many different kinds of laws.

But there are other laws that are invisible to us—visible only to God—which control the Kingdom of Heaven. A miracle is basically the imposition of the laws of the Kingdom of Heaven over the laws of this world.

What activates these higher laws remains a mystery. There are certain factors which often set them in motion. Prayer, for instance.

Prayer is not necessarily a group of people getting together and fasting and waiting on God, then asking God to meet their need. Nor is it somebody standing up in an auditorium and praying vocally. Prayer has many different kinds of connotations. In basic form prayer is, as James Montgomery said, "the soul's sincere desire." God listens to the heart. So prayer seems to be one of the things that keys off miracles.

Faith is another element which seems to be important in laying the foundation for miracles to happen. Jesus loved to ask people if they believed He could perform a miracle. For instance, when two blind men came to Him crying, "Have mercy on us, Son of David." Jesus turned and asked, "Do you believe that I am able to do this?"

"Yes, Lord," they replied.

He then touched their eyes and they were able to see. His explanation: "According to your faith will it be done to you" (cf. Matthew 9:27-31).

Yet we find miracles happening to people who don't believe, just as we find miracles happening to folks who don't pray. Therefore, at the heart of every miracle is the providence and the goodness and the faithfulness of God.

Faith, human desire, radical circumstances, the taking of spiritual authority . . . all of these can play a part. Yet in the long run we are still subject to the sovereignty of

God, and it is God alone who makes the final decision—sometimes totally apart from even the prerequisites set in Scripture.

But there are certain factors that put certain miracles into effect at certain times. It is up to us to discern these, for it is obvious God intends for miracles to be as much in evidence today as they were when Jesus was here in the flesh—and He wants them to occur through us. He wants us to be people who are not just governed by the laws of this universe, but governed by the laws of the Kingdom of God.

The Bible tells us we need to walk in both realms. We must obey the laws here. We can't get out on the highway and drive 120 miles an hour just because our speedometer says we can and believe that God will miraculously take us through the heavy traffic. He wants to work in balance with the laws of this world as well as with the higher laws of the Kingdom. There may be a time, for instance, when we need to drive over the speed limit for the sake of saving someone's life. There may be a time when we need to pick up a poisonous snake—or are bitten by one accidentally. God does not give us license to pick up snakes to test our faith, any more than He gives us license to drive recklessly. But we need to remember He is a God of miracles, and if He has given us a commission—as He gave Paul when He told him to go to Rome—then no poisonous snake will thwart us as we carry it out.

Now we come to look at one of the most exciting stories in the Bible. It is not only a story of a wonderful miracle, it is the story of a miracle that breaks all the rules. Let's look at the cast of characters who gather around Jesus.

THE MAN BLIND FROM BIRTH: This is the only miracle in the Gospels in which the sufferer is said to have been afflicted from birth. Twice in the book of Acts we read stories of people helpless from birth. One was the lame man at the Beautiful Gate of the Temple who was begging for alms. To him Peter and John said, "Silver and gold I do not have, but what I have I give you. In the name of Jesus Christ of Nazareth, walk" (Acts 3:1-10). The other was the story of the impotent man at Lystra (Acts 14:8).

This blind man, however, was something of a fixture in the Jerusalem society. A sidewalk beggar, he had been around for a long time, sitting beside the road with a cup and pleading for money. Unlike the beggar Jesus healed at the Pool of Bethesda, this fellow was articulate—with a sharp wit and even sharper tongue (which we discover when the religious authorities begin quizzing him). But he doesn't know who Jesus is, and unlike Blind Bartimaeus in Jericho who was also a roadside beggar, he had never heard that Jesus was a miracle-worker. Therefore, he didn't even ask for healing. In fact, he seemed to be getting along rather well inside his severe limitations of poverty and blindness.

JESUS' DISCIPLES: As Jesus and His disciples were walking down the street, they saw the blind man. The disciples asked Jesus a theological question: "Rabbi, who sinned, this man or his parents, that he was born blind?" (John 9:2).

The disciples had no interest in the man's blindness. Blindness was common in the days of Jesus due to the high rate of eye disease—a condition that still exists in the desert regions of the Far East. The disciples were interested in the theology behind his blindness. They simply saw this as a good time to get an answer to a question which had bothered Jews since the time of Job—and which remains in people's minds to this day: Who is responsible for affliction?

The Jews believed all suffering was the result of sin—of someone's sin. Disease, therefore, was caused either by the individual or by his parents.

We ask, "How could a man have sinned if he was born blind?" But the Jews of that day believed in the preexistence of the soul. This was not a biblical concept. Indeed, the Bible teaches that each of us is unique, and while God foreknew our lives, we came into being at conception—not at the creation of all things. The concept of preexistence—and the resulting theory of reincarnation—was a Greek concept, one the Jews had picked up from Plato. Perhaps the Jews of Jesus' day believed a man born blind picked up his affliction from some sin he committed in his former life. If it wasn't that, they reasoned, it must have been his parents who sinned. That idea, by the way, is legitimate and is woven throughout the thought of the Old Testament: "I, the Lord Thy God, am a jealous God, visiting the iniquity of the fathers upon the children unto the third and fourth generations" (Exodus 20:5 [KJV]; 34:7; and Numbers 14:18). "May the iniquity of his fathers be remembered before the Lord and may the sin of his mother never be blotted out" (Psalm 109:14).

There are many references throughout the Old Testament to support this concept. Indeed, we all inherit to a great degree the sins of our fathers. It's not uncommon for a father or a mother who lives in sin to conceive and give birth to a child which will carry for life the scars of that sin. Heroin addiction, cocaine addiction, syphilis, even heavy smoking by a mother—all these can maim and deform a child for life.

The two primary factors which affect us are heredity and environment. Millions of children are born innocently into this world bearing the results of their parents' sin. It is one of the tonic chords of the Old Testament that no man lives to himself and no man dies to himself. When a person sins, he sets in motion an hereditary train of consequences which in later generations can be ended only when someone breaks the curse by taking authority in the name of Jesus.

JESUS, THE SON OF GOD: Jesus answered His disciples' question by saying, "Neither this man nor his parents sinned." That's not to say they were sinless. He was simply saying the blindness was not caused by sin but "so that the work of God might be displayed in his life."

Then He goes ahead and preaches to them a little bit: "As long as it is day, we must do the work of Him who sent Me. Night is coming, when no one can work. While I am in the world, I am the light of the world."

Then He pauses for a moment, letting that soak in. The question, He is implying, is not who is at fault, but who is going to do something about it. It's the problem we all face. We get so caught up in the debate over causes we forget that the real problem is our powerlessness to do anything about it. And we forget that the desire of God is to work a miracle.

The Jews were great debaters. They loved to argue— especially over theological issues. The rabbis would sit for days debating history, the law, proper behavior, the nature of God, the Talmud . . . on and on. The Pharisees and scribes would debate also, but their arguments often grew violent—sometimes physical. "Put two Jews in a room, ask them a question and you'll get three opinions," the old rabbis joke. And so it is, even today.

"If you want a theological answer," Jesus said, "here it is. I'm going to demonstrate how God can be glorified through this. That's something which defies debate."

Remember: The purpose of miracles is to glorify God. When Matthew, Mark, and Luke wrote their biographies of Jesus—just a few years after His ascension—they made a point (Matthew in particular) that Jesus was often moved with compassion. They imply that compassion for suffering mankind was the primary motivation for Jesus' miracles. But John, writing many years later, has had a chance to understand far more of the nature of God. He gives an added dimension. He does not rule out compassion, but he points out that the primary purpose of the healings and miracles was the glorification of God.

Remember, also, that miracles are the exhibition of one law overriding another law. In this case, it is not only the imposition of the higher law of love over the physical law that says that once a man is born blind, he remains that way. Jesus also went a step beyond and overrode the religious laws of the day. He healed on the Sabbath.

THE PHARISEES: Every religious community has its fundamentalists, the right-wingers. The Pharisees were the fundamentalists of the Jews. They did more than hold to orthodox doctrine and live pious lives—they felt mandated to see that everyone else did, also. They felt, as God's representatives on earth (His only representatives, they said), that they were to take up the offense for God. Thus, if anyone did anything which violated the law, they were offended. If they felt anyone was attacking God or God's law, they were compelled to rise to the defense, killing if necessary to protect the law.

The Pharisees strictly avoided contact with anything which could make them ritually impure. They exercised great care in matters of ritual purity, in food laws, and the Sabbath law. Their piety centered around the study of biblical law, in the course of which they built up a body of traditional interpretation called the Oral law which tended to assume a role of importance equal to that of the Written law itself. The Written law or law of Moses, called the Pentateuch (the first five books of the Old Testament), was the heart of their belief; but the Talmud, the interpretation of these laws by ancient rabbis, was—to them—equally inspired.

The Pharisees enjoyed considerable prestige among the people. This was partly because many of them originally came from humble backgrounds, unlike the Sadducean artistocracy, and partly because they had not been afraid to make a stand for their principles. For example, they did not shrink from publicly opposing Herod the Great when he trampled on traditional Jewish ways, even though this cost many of them their lives—as when they removed the figure of the eagle which Herod had set up over the entrance to the Temple but which they considered to be idolatrous.

At the time of Christ, the Jewish nation was under Roman domination. Unlike the Zealots, however, the Pharisees resisted the popular movement of revolt. They preferred to cooperate with the Roman authorities as long as those authorities could be used to further their means.

Although Jesus commended the Pharisees for their dedication to the law, He was quick to point out they had missed the real point of the law. They adhered to the letter of the law while having no idea of the spirit in which it was given. They knew the law, but not the Lawgiver. They were more interested in keeping the law than glorifying God. The Sabbath, Jesus told them, was made for man—but they had made man a servant to their concepts of the Sabbath law. The law, to them, was more important than humankind. Thus, when they found a woman in adultery they were eager to stone her to death, saying the law was more important than forgiveness. If they could not find some legal reason to do the actual killing, they were shrewd enough to incite a riot and let someone else do the killing while they stood by, holding the clothes of the executioners as did Paul at the death of Stephen (Acts 7:58)—legally innocent but morally guilty.

THE BLIND MAN'S PARENTS: This couple played minor, but important, roles in the drama. They were caught in the eternal struggle of wanting to help and defend their son, wanting to rejoice over his miraculous healing, wanting to be grateful to the miracle-worker who had done this wonderful thing to him; but pressured by the system of the Pharisees, knowing that any approval of Jesus would mean they would be thrown out of their place of religious security—the synagogue. In the end, they shrugged away all responsibility by saying, "You'll have to get your answers from our son; we know nothing."

THE MIRACLE: The method of the miracle was simple. Jesus spit in the dust of the path, molded the moist earth into mud, and wiped it on the eyes of the blind man. Then He told him to go to the nearby Pool of Siloam and wash his eyes. When the man did as he was told, he could instantly see.

The use of spittle seems repulsive and unhygienic to us in the western world, but in ancient times people believed spittle had healing qualities. The Greeks, in particular, believed there was magical power in spittle, especially what they called "fasting spit." (Those who have done any fasting know there is a difference between fasting spit and eating spit.) There were many legends that accompanied the use of spit. If an important person spit on an unimportant person, good things were supposed to happen. But if an unimportant person were to spit on an important person, he might lose his head. Sometimes it was an honor to be spit on by an important dignitary because of the medicinal powers and the blessings that accompanied the act.

Pliny, the famous Roman journalist, collected what was

then called "scientific information." He wrote an entire chapter on the use of spittle. He believed it was a sovereign preservative against poisonous serpents, epilepsy, and leprous spots.

Jesus knew the theories and superstitions of the day. Rather than make fun of or refute the theories, He worked inside them to perform the miraculous acts of God. He didn't do it the way the Greeks would have done it. They would have wanted Him to simply spit into the eyes of the blind man. Of course, Jesus could have done it that way, or He could have simply spoken and said, "Receive your sight," as He did with other blind men on other occasions. Instead, He spit on the ground, made mud, and rubbed that in the blind man's eyes. By mixing the spit with dirt He contaminated the Grecian concept. By making mud on the Sabbath, which was forbidden by the Jewish law, He offended the Pharisees.

He then told the man to go to the nearby Pool of Siloam and wash his eyes. When the man obeyed, he was able to see for the first time in his life.

The Pool of Siloam was one of the landmarks of Jerusalem. It was located just inside the Water Gate which opened out over the Kidron Valley. There, deep in the valley at the foot of the City of David, was the Spring Gihon, sometimes called the Virgin's Fountain. The location of the spring was perhaps the major factor in the selection of the site of Jerusalem 3000 years before the birth of Jesus. Its water was always vital to the city's survival. To that spring had been built a staircase of thirty-three rock-cut steps leading down to it. There, from the stone basin, people drew water. But since the spring was outside the city wall, it was completely exposed and could be cut off in the event of a military siege, making the city's water supply vulnerable.

In the year 701 B.C., King Hezekiah, fearing an attack

by the Assyrian Empire, told his engineers to design a way to get water from the spring into the city without having to carry it through the Water Gate. It was a critical time. Sennacherib, king of Assyria, had overwhelmed all the other fortified cities in Judah and was now marching against Jerusalem. Back in Nineveh, the capital of Assyria, the king's royal scribe, confident of another victory by Sennacherib, chiseled his version of the yet-to-come victory on the wall of the palace. "As for Hezekiah the Judean," he wrote, "he did not submit to my yoke . . . I shut him up in Jerusalem his residence like a bird in its cage."

And that's what would have happened if Hezekiah's engineers had failed. But they didn't. In one of the most remarkable engineering feats in history, Hezekiah's engineers designed a tunnel to bring the water under the city wall and into a pool called Sent (the water being "sent" from the Spring Gihon to the pool inside the city). However, the engineers did not have much time to dig the tunnel, which was through solid rock. Therefore they began their digging and cutting from both ends—one group of miners starting at the Spring Gihon and the other at the Pool Sent. If the engineers had cut straight it would have been a distance of 366 yards. But instead they cut in a zig-gag or S-shaped pattern at a length of 583 yards—perhaps to avoid sacred sites or to follow a fissure in the rock. That makes the tunnel even more of an engineering miracle, for when the two teams came together they were only inches off course. After its completion, the old outlet at Gihon was sealed and hidden from view.

Just days after the tunnel was completed, Sennacherib attacked. It was a vicious siege, and the story is told in detail in 2 Chronicles 32:1-21, 30; Isaiah 22:9-11; and 2 Kings 20:20. With the help of an angel, Sennacherib was soundly defeated and later killed by his own sons. Hezekiah lived on, was later healed miraculously, and finally died an honorable death. His tunnel remains to this day and can be walked from its origin to the old Pool Sent—which in Jesus' day was called Siloam.

In 1880 a young boy discovered a 77-word inscription chiseled into the tunnel wall where the two teams of diggers met. It describes how the miners heard each others' voices through a crack in the rock: "When the tunnel was driven through, the tunnelers hewed the rock, each man towards his fellow, pick-axe against pick-axe. And the water flowed from the spring towards the reservoir for twelve hundred cubits."

It was to this pool Jesus sent the blind man to wash his eyes. Even that act had meaning. The Pool of Siloam was the place the rabbis drew the water for ceremonial cleansing in the Temple. Thus, when Jesus sent this man to the Pool of Siloam He was following Jewish custom, working inside the framework of the customs of the day.

There was one significant difference, however. When the Jews washed with ceremonial water, they remained the same. When this man washed, he came up seeing. The difference was the touch of Jesus.

The actual physical miracle stops when the man receives his sight. But the intrigue continues with the rest of the passage.

> *The man's neighbors and those who had formerly seen him begging asked, "Isn't this the same man who used to sit and beg?"*
>
> *Some claimed he was. Others argued, "No, he only looks like him."*
>
> *But the man himself claimed, "I am the man."*
>
> *"How then were your eyes opened?" they demanded.*
>
> *He replied, "The man they call Jesus made some mud and put it on my eyes."*

I love it! He didn't say, "God miraculously healed me." He said, "This dude came down the road and put mud in my eye." That's a good, honest answer. Everybody could understand that. No spiritual, religious talk, just an honest, open response.

> "He told me to go to Siloam and wash. So I went, washed, and now I can see."
> "Where is this man?" they asked him. "I don't know," he said.

At that point his neighbors determined they better involve the experts, so they took the man to the Pharisees. That was a mistake, for now the religious hierarchy was involved, and with it all the vested interests of threatened leaders.

> Now the day on which Jesus had made the mud and opened the man's eyes was a Sabbath.

That spelled trouble. Forget that the man was able to see. Forget that a mightly miracle had occurred. All they could see was that one of their laws had been broken. If they allowed Jesus to get away with it, He, or others, might start breaking laws on a wholesale basis—and they would be out of a job. So they tried to charge Jesus as a law-breaker—making mud on the Sabbath.

Undoubtedly, He had broken the law. In fact, He had broken it in three different ways.

(1) By making mud, He was guilty of working on the Sabbath. The Jews, by trying to interpret the letter of the law of Moses, had gone far beyond God's intent. For instance, a man was not allowed to wear sandals shod with nails on the Sabbath, since the weight of the nails would constitute a burden, and it was forbidden to carry

a burden on the Sabbath. A man could not cut his finger-nails or pull a single hair from his head since this constituted work—and it was forbidden to work on the Sabbath. Obviously, to make mud was a major violation.

(2) Jesus broke the law by healing on the Sabbath. A person could receive medical attention only if his life was at stake—and then the only medical help he was allowed to receive was to keep him from getting worse. To receive medical help which would make him better was work on the part of the physician or healer. It was forbidden to set a broken limb on the Sabbath. A man with a toothache could not suck vinegar through his teeth. The law said, "If a man's hand or foot is dislocated he may not pour cold water over it." The cold water might help heal the injury, and for that the man should wait until the Sabbath was over at sundown on Saturday. To give sight to a man born blind was a clear violation of the law. If anything could wait one more day, that could.

(3) The Sabbath law was even more specific. In regards to fasting, the law stated, "As to fasting spittle, it is not lawful to put it so much as upon the eyelids."

By observing all these rules, the Pharisees sought to honor God. Jesus, however, believed the law was written to serve man, not man the law. Therefore, any act of mercy on the Sabbath would have pleased God, not offended Him.

Jesus had deliberately broken the Sabbath law in order to honor God.

Unfortunately the Pharisees are typical of people of every generation, including ours, who condemn all who do not believe as they believe, who condemn all who approach God any way other than their own way. Every one of us to some degree has a pharisaical spirit. If we see someone doing something different from the way we do it, there is a tendency on our part to say our way is better. Even though I may tolerate what another does, in my heart I still believe he is wrong. If others were right, they would do things as I do them—the right way.

> Some of the Pharisees said, "This man is not from God, for He does not keep the Sabbath," But others asked, "How can a sinner do such miraculous signs?" So they were divided.

The Jews believed God heard only the prayers of a good man. That's basic throughout Jewish law: God does not hear the prayers of a bad man. (Note: It is of interest that just a few years ago a fundamentalist Christian leader stated publicly that he did not believe God heard the prayers of a Jew—causing a violent controversy which lasted a number of months.) The Jews determined who was good by who kept the law. If you kept the law you were good; if you didn't keep the law you were bad.

So they said, "Jesus has just broken the law; therefore, He must be a bad man." But then there was the fact of the miracle. "Only a good man can perform miracles," some argued. "Therefore, He must be good."

Finally they turned to the blind man. After all, it was his eyes that were opened. "What have you to say about Him?" they challenged.

The man's reply was simple. "He is a prophet."

That answer really infuriated the Pharisees. The blind man probably didn't know what a prophet was, but it seemed to him to be a pretty good thing to call Jesus.

Unable to receive satisfaction, the Pharisees sent for the man's parents.

> "Is this your son?" they asked. "Is this the one you say was born blind? How is it that now he can see?"

There was one thing the Pharisees could do which was fearsome above all things. They had the power to turn a person out of the synagogue. By doing so, they denied the banished person the presence of God. They denied him forgiveness of sin. They denied him the atonement. The person turned out of the synagogue was totally lost and considered worse than the leper. The blind man's parents knew that if they displeased the Pharisees, they would be turned out of the synagogue. It was a sad conflict, for they wanted to support their son, but were afraid of the consequences.

The picture is classic: a little Jewish mother and a wimpy husband wearing his yarmulke, standing before the mighty robed Pharisees.

"Is this your son?" the Pharisees ask. The parents study the question a moment. Finally the father carefully answers, "We know he is our son, and we know he was born blind. But how he can see now, or who opened his eyes, we don't know. Ask him. He is of age."

In other words, "Don't involve me. Let him speak for himself."

The Pharisees were getting nowhere. In desperation they sent for the man one more time. "Give glory to God," they said. "We know this man Jesus is a sinner."

It's interesting how they tied those two things together: give glory to God by condemning somebody else. But the man's answer refuted all argument. It was the ultimate witness.

> He replied, "Whether He is a sinner or not, I don't know. One thing I do know. I was blind but now I see!"

He left absolutely no room for argument. How can you argue with the result? "I don't care who did it," he said.

"I don't care how He did it. The important thing is this:
I have been blind all my life, and now I can see. I may
not like what I'm looking at, but I can see. How do you
argue with that?"

These men were experts at arguing. But there is
absolutely no way you can argue with a miracle.

> *Then they asked him, "What did He do to you? How
> did He open your eyes?"*
> *He answered, "I have told you already and you did
> not listen. Why do you want to hear it again? Do you
> want to become His disciples, too?"*

It was more than they could take. They turned to
personal insult and did to him what his parents were afraid
they would do to them. Irony of ironies, instead of rejoicing
over his healing, they turned him out of the synagogue.

> *Jesus heard that they had thrown him out, and when
> He found him, He said, "Do you believe in the Son
> of Man [or Messiah]?" "Who is He, sir?" the man asked.
> "Tell me so that I may believe in Him."*

Remember, this is the first time the man had seen Jesus,
although he had heard His voice and felt His touch before
he was healed. But Jesus had sent him to the Pool of
Siloam and the man had not seen Him since he received
his sight.

> *Jesus said, "You have now seen Him; in fact, He
> is the one speaking with you."*

Suddenly the man received a second sight—healed not
from physical blindness, but from spiritual blindness.
"Lord, I believe," he said. Then he worshiped Jesus.

This is one of the few times Jesus comes right out and says He is the Messiah. But the occasion was so pure, and the man's desire so untainted, that Jesus felt safe in saying, "You are looking at the Son of God."

Who were the real blind men? One of the Pharisees angrily but correctly assessed the situation when he blurted out: "What? Are we blind too?"

Jesus replied, "If you were blind, you would not be guilty of sin; but now that you claim you can see, your guilt remains."

Jesus points out that knowledge demands action. The Pharisees knew the law, but by not acting on it they had disobeyed God and were what they accused the others of being—sinners. Unto whom much is given, Jesus said in another place, much will be required. We, like the Pharisees, have received much. Now God is requiring that we give what we have received—testimony of our own healing. In the name of Jesus we are to then give healing to others.

Father, I pray that Your miracles of yesterday will be real in our lives today. I pray for men and women who are not afraid to do the ridiculous, who will reach out and touch the eyes of others, that they too may see. In Jesus' name. Amen.

SEVEN

HOPE FOR THE HOPELESS
Jesus Heals a Leper

Jesus reached out His hand and touched the man . . . ."Be clean!" Immediately he was cured of his leprosy.

MATTHEW 8:1-4
(also Mark 1:40-42; Luke 5:12-15)

When He came down from the mountainside, large crowds followed Him. A man with leprosy came and knelt before Him and said, "Lord, if You are willing, You can make me clean."

Jesus reached out His hand and touched the man. "I am willing," He said. "Be clean!" Immediately he was cured of his leprosy. Then Jesus said to him, "See that you don't tell anyone. But go, show yourself to the priest and offer the gift Moses commanded, as a testimony to them."

Leprosy, or as it is often called now, Hansen's disease, is one of the most terrible diseases of all times. No other sickness—except for the new disease of AIDS—can draw life from a person with such calculated cruelty.

In Jesus' day, leprosy was known as "the living death." E.W.G. Masterman, in his article on the disease in the *Dictionary of Christ and the Gospels*, says, "No other disease reduces a human being for so many years to so hideous a wreck."

149

There are two kinds of leprosy. The first is known as *nodular* or *tubercular leprosy*. It begins with an extreme weariness accompanied by pains in the joints. Shortly after that, the skin, especially on the back and face, begins to discolor with symmetrical patches. On these patches form nodules, at first pink, then turning brown. They grow into thick, glossy, tumor-like welts. The skin thickens and the nodules spread to the folds of the cheek, the nose, the lips, and the forehead. Over a period of time the entire face may lose its human appearance. As the tumors grow larger they begin to ulcerate, discharging a foul smelling liquid. The eyebrows fall out; the eyes become fixed; and as the ulcers spread to the larynx, the voice becomes hoarse and the patient wheezes as he breathes. In time, the hands and feet ulcerate until the leper becomes a mass of oozing tumors. The suffered becomes despicable both to others and to himself. The average patient eventually loses his ability to think correctly and dies within nine years.

The second type of leprosy is *anesthetic leprosy*. It begins in a similar way, but in this form, the nerve trunks are affected. The leprous area loses all sensation. The victim may not be aware of this until he burns or cuts his hand or foot and realizes there is no sensation of pain. The muscles deteriorate and the tendons contract until the hands become like claws. The hands, feet, nose, and ears ulcerate as the disease progresses until, in the end, hands and feet may drop off and the patient may be without a nose and ears. The patient may live as long as 30 years after becoming infected before he dies a horrible death. On occasion, nodular and anesthetic leprosy are mixed.

Although Hansen's disease is now curable and known to be virtually non-communicable, in Jesus' day it was known as the curse of Satan—the worst thing that could happen to any human being.

Leprosy and many other skin diseases were (and are)

common in the Middle East. Lepers were pointedly mentioned in the Levitical law (Leviticus 13-14), and distinction was made between leprosy and various other skin diseases. The desire to protect the people from the disease was understandable, but the penalty the law placed on the sick person was almost unbearable. The leper, regardless of sex, age, or status in the community, was to be examined by the priest and, if found to have leprosy, banished from the community. "The person with such an infectious disease must wear torn clothes, let his hair be unkempt, cover the lower part of his face and cry out, 'Unclean! Unclean!' As long as he has the infection he remains unclean. He must live alone; he must live outside the camp" (Leviticus 13:45-46).

In Jesus' day, the rules regarding lepers had multiplied from the simple regulations set forth in Leviticus. Of the 61 different contacts the law listed which could defile the proper Jew, being touched by or touching a leper was second in severity only to touching a dead body. Thus, the leper was barred from Jerusalem and all walled towns. If a leper put his head through the door or window of a house or building, that building was declared "unclean"—even to the roof beams. It was illegal to greet or speak to a leper. No one might come closer than six feet (four cubits). If a leper was upwind from a Jew, he had to stand at least 150 feet away. People, including the rabbis, often threw stones at the leper, much as they would at a mangy dog, to keep him away.

In the Middle Ages, many of these regulations were adopted by the church as well. A leper was declared spiritually dead. He had to wear a black garment so all might recognize him as unclean. He was forced to live with other lepers in a leper house. He was not allowed to attend church services but could peer through a "squint" hole in the wall while the service went on.

The Jewish historian, Josephus, tells us that lepers were treated "as if they were, in effect, dead men." Dr. A.B. MacDonald, writing of the African leper colony where he worked, said, "The leper is sick in mind as well as body. For some reason there is an attitude to leprosy different from the attitude to any other disfiguring disease. It is associated with shame and horror, and carries, in some mysterious way, a sense of guilt, although innocently acquired like most contagious troubles. Shunned and despised, frequently do lepers consider taking their own lives, and some do."

As horrible as the physical disease was, then, the emotional destruction was equally great. Banished. Unclean. Defiled. Declared spiritually dead. No disease in history has separated the patient from society as has leprosy. The leper was hated by others, believed himself to be hated by God, and so hated himself.

It was such a man who came to Jesus, asking for help.

> When He came down from the mountainside, large crowds followed Him. A man with leprosy came and knelt before Him and said, "Lord, if You are willing, You can make me clean."

The leper approached Jesus with a certain confidence that was rare in those days. He had no doubt that if Jesus willed, He could make him clean. It was an exhibition of incredible faith. No leper was allowed near a rabbi. The penalty was stoning. Yet for some reason this man seemed to have perfect confidence in Jesus' power. Remember, leprosy was the one disease for which there was no prescribed rabbinic remedy. But this man was certain Jesus could do what no one else could do—heal him.

This is always the first step in the healing process—

will. It's difficult to believe, but doctors who deal with lepers have told me that in the progression of the disease, one of the first things to go is the will to get well. Lepers quickly fall into a type of hopelessness that destroys even the desire to get well. As a result, even when medical treatment is offered, many refuse it. The sickness not only destroys the tissues of the body, but the attitudes of the mind.

This leper not only came with confidence, he approached Jesus with reverence and humility. He did not demand his healing. He did not say, "You've healed others; I want to claim what is rightfully mine." He said, "If You will, You can cleanse me." He realized he had been declared a dead man. He was a nobody in the eyes of all the people—especially the religious people. But he recognized Jesus as a non-religious man of God— something nobody in Israel had ever seen before. He was saying, "I know that men will flee from me and have nothing to do with me; I know You have the right to throw stones at me; but I also know You have the power of God in You—the power to heal me if You want to."

The text says the leper came and "knelt before Him." The King James Bible says he "worshiped" Jesus. The Greek verb is *proskunein*—a word never used for anything but *worship of the gods*. Somehow this leper knew that Jesus was the Son of God. That was the reason he was able to approach with such confidence. He knew God was a God of miracles.

> *Jesus reached out His hand and touched the man. "I am willing," He said. "Be clean!" Immediately he was cured of his leprosy.*

Nothing like that had ever happened before. That a man, any man, should touch a leper was as unthinkable as a man reaching down and picking up a poisonous snake

by the tail. Yet it was exactly these two signs that God
had given Moses 1200 years before when He called him
to return to Egypt and lead His people into freedom. To
prove to Moses that He was a God of miracles, Jehovah
had selected two signs. In the first sign He told Moses
to throw his staff to the ground. "Moses threw it on the
ground and it became a snake, and he ran from it" (Exodus
4:3). God then told Moses to pick it up—by the tail. Moses
was terrified, but when he obeyed, the serpent was
transformed back into his staff. The second sign was even
more significant. "Then the Lord said, 'Put your hand
inside your cloak.' So Moses put his hand into his cloak,
and when he took it out, was was leprous, like snow. 'Now
put it back into your cloak,' He said. So Moses put his
hand back into his cloak, and when he took it out, it was
restored, like the rest of his flesh" (Exodus 4:6-7). The
serpent was the symbol of danger, leprosy the symbol of
disease and sin. As easily as God could change a serpent
into a staff, so He could heal disease and forgive sin.

Jesus exhibited this when He did the unthinkable and
touched the leper—bringing instant healing.

The law said Jesus must not touch a leper. To do so
would render Jesus ceremonially unclean. Jesus paid no
attention to the law. The law of lepers was designed to
protect people from infection. Jesus, the miracle-worker,
overrode the natural system by saying the power of God
was greater than the power of infection.

Jesus had but one obligation in life—to help the
hopeless. If it was the law that brought hopelessness, Jesus
overrode the law of Moses with the law of love, saying
He was not breaking the law, but fulfilling it. If it was
disease which brought hopelessness, Jesus overrode the
natural laws of infection and brought healing. If it was
demons which brought hopelessness, Jesus took spiritual
authority over those dark citizens of the underworld and

cast them out of those people trying to find God. He was not fearful of demons, infection, or the law. There was only one law—the law of love. The duty of compassion, the obligation of love took precedence over all other rules, laws, and regulations.

No compassionate doctor sees a sick child as a menace; rather, he sees a hurting child needing to be helped. No loving parent, seeing his helpless child about to be attacked by a poisonous snake, hesitates to combat the serpent. The law of love rules in such situations. The true child of God will break any convention and will take any risk to help a fellowman in need.

Jesus did not see the leper as infectious, nor as ceremonially unclean. He saw him as God saw him—a human soul in desperate need.

Many years ago I was desperately searching for spiritual reality. Sadly, I had not found it in the churches. Instead I had found a certain religious cruelty, a modern day pharisaism which declared flawed people like myself "unclean." In fact, once my moral imperfections had been discovered, I had been voted out of two churches. Like the lepers of Jesus' day, I had been told to move outside the wall and never return. In the eyes of the self-righteous, I was as a dead man.

Yet, like this leper, I never lost faith in God. I sensed that the Jesus of yesterday was still alive. I believed in His church, even though it was as flawed as I. I longed to see some evidence of His supernatural power—evidence which had been denied me by my theological tradition which taught there were no more miracles except those wrought by science and coincidence.

Then one rainy, November afternoon, I was roaming through the ghetto section of Brooklyn known as Fort Green—a haven for street gangs and heroin addicts. My guide was a young Puerto Rican named Nicky Cruz who had formerly led a gang called the Mau Maus. The story of Nicky's conversion under the ministry of David Wilkerson had been vividly told by John Sherrill in Wilkerson's book, *The Cross and the Switchblade*. I was now writing Nicky's story for a book we would call *Run Baby Run*, and Nicky was taking me to his former haunts in Brooklyn.

That afternoon we had gone upstairs in the Teen Challenge building where Nicky had once lived. The old, two-story house was a rehabilitation center for drug addicts and street criminals. Nicky had worked there under David Wilkerson after he had gone to Bible school and entered a full-time ministry.

After walking through the upstairs portion of the building, we came back down the long, narrow flight of stairs which ended near the front door. Nicky was in front of me as we descended the stairs. As we reached the bottom step, he paused. I looked over his shoulder and saw that a heroin addict had dragged himself in out of the rain toward the receptionist's desk, which was momentarily unmanned, and collapsed on the bottom step. I could not tell how old the pathetic boy was. His face was buried in the stained carpet of the step. His flimsy shirt was wet, sticking to the skin of his back. He was retching, trying to vomit, but it was only dry heaves. His entire body seemed to be convulsing as he went into the spasms of drug withdrawal. I saw all that in a moment, but the thing that registered most were the running sores on his head and the back of his neck. Nicky reached out and put his hand on the back of the man's head and began to pray. He used a language I did not understand. But it was not the prayer language which struck me— it was Nicky's fearless compassion. While I was shrinking up against the wall, he was reaching out with love toward someone who was where he had once been. As he prayed, the man turned his head to the side and relaxed on the steps. Instantly the heaving and vomiting stopped. It was as if the man had gone to sleep.

The prayer only lasted 15 to 20 seconds. By that time two attendants had arrived. They helped the man to his feet and took him up the stairs to a bed. I discovered later that the healing had been instantaneous. The effects of the drugs had been nullified by the power of God. There was no "cold turkey" withdrawal, just a long period of sleep followed by several weeks of regaining his strength and allowing his skin to heal.

It was the first time I had seen an instant answer to prayer since I had been a small child, praying the forest fire would not burn our home down. But it was not the miracle which convinced me God was still alive, living and ministering through His people on earth. It was the compassion. When I saw Nicky place his hand on those running sores, I saw Jesus touching the leper.

And I knew God was alive.

Today we are faced with a crisis a million times worse than drug addiction, far worse than leprosy. Although I believe medical science will eventually discover a cure for the deadly epidemic called AIDS (Acquired Immune Deficiency Syndrome), at this writing there is no known cure. The disease is 40 times as deadly as the deadliest diseases heretofore known. There is no cure and no vaccine. Dr. John Seale of the British Royal Society of Medicine called AIDS "the molecular-biological equivalent of the nuclear bomb," saying it "has the capability to wipe out the entire human race." Spread primarily through homosexual activity and by drug addicts who use "dirty needles," it can also be acquired by coming into contact with the body fluids of infected people—especially blood and saliva.

As the epidemic spreads, followers of Christ are being

forced to reevaluate their faith. How should individual believers react when confronted with an AIDS patient? What should a church do when an AIDS victim wants to attend the services? Do we lay on hands? If we do, should we wear surgical gloves? Dare we drink communion from a common cup? First Corinthians 11:28-30 says each Christian should "examine *himself* before he . . . drinks of the cup." It says nothing of examining your neighbor.

The only healing of an AIDS patient that I know of (I am certain there are others) took place at the altar rail of our church in early 1987. The son of one of our spiritual family had rebelled against the teachings of his father and mother and adopted a lifestyle which exposed him to the virus. Shortly afterwards he was infected. The disease spread rapidly. The doctors in our local hospital told his father the boy's internal organs were destroyed. They did not expect the young man to live more than another week.

People from our church visited him in the hospital. His father and mother encouraged him to submit himself for prayer. He was temporarily released from the hospital to attend one of the morning church services. Only a few weeks before I had challenged the people to be prepared— that AIDS patients were going to seek us out, just as lepers came to Jesus. The young man, gaunt, almost lifeless, came to the altar that morning. The elders of the church gathered around him. Without hesitation ten good men reached out and put their hands on him, taking authority over the infections in his body. We anointed him with oil, using James 5:14-15 as our authority. "Is any one of you sick? He should call the elders of the church to pray over him and anoint him with oil in the name of the Lord. And the prayer offered in faith will make the sick person well; the Lord will raise him up. If he has sinned, he will be forgiven."

The next day the young man returned to the hospital.

By the end of the week the doctors had diagnosed him
free from the virus. Only a few days later he was released.

Bottom line: Christians must run the risk of infection
by ministering to those who come for help. Remember,
Jesus promises protection (Mark 16:18) if we are forced
to handle snakes or drink poison. As Jesus touched this
leper, so God's people are called to reach out and touch
all who are hopeless. Healing comes only when we are
willing to lay down our lives for others.

> Then Jesus said to him, "See that you don't tell anyone.
> But go, show yourself to the priest and offer the gift
> Moses commanded, as a testimony to them."

There were proper channels for the confirmation of
a healing in the biblical period. Jesus did not want to
deliberately antagonize the priests in the Temple. For the
most part, they were doing the best they could to serve
God with their limited vision and understanding. Instead,
He realized this would be a wonderful opportunity to
glorify God as a God of miracles among the religious
leaders.

Even though there was a complicated ceremony outlined
in Leviticus 14 to declare a leper clean, it was seldom
used except in the case of skin diseases, for leprosy was
considered hopeless. There was no known cure. Jesus had
pointed this out at the beginning of His public ministry
when He stood in the synagogue at Nazareth and read
from the prophet Isaiah, proclaiming Himself the Messiah.
In His explanation to the people He said, "And there
were many in Israel with leprosy in the time of Elisha
the prophet, yet not one of them was cleansed—only
Naaman the Syrian" (Luke 4:27).

The reference is to a remarkable story in 2 Kings 5.
Naaman, the king of Syria, had leprosy. Humbling himself,

he came to the Jewish prophet, Elisha, asking for help. Elisha told him to dip himself in the Jordan River seven times. He did, and was healed. It was another evidence of God's miraculous healing power.

When Jesus reminded the Jews in Nazareth of this, and in so doing let them know that He had the same power as Elisha, they tried to kill Him. No mortal, they knew, had the power to cure leprosy. Only God could do that.

Jesus wanted the priests in the Temple to know God was curing leprosy. He warned the man to be careful not to tell anyone else, for He did not want the people to try to force Him to become a military Messiah. Instead, Jesus encouraged the man to use the proper and accepted (although never used) procedure for ceremonial cleansing.

The ceremony of restoration from "unclean" to "clean" was complicated, but filled with beautiful symbolism. The man had to present himself to the priest for a physical examination, bringing with him two birds. One of these was killed over running water. The living bird was then dipped in the blood of the dead bird, along with cedar, scarlet, and hyssop—and allowed to fly free. The man then washed himself and shaved, changed his clothes, and seven days later presented himself again for examination of his skin. This time he sacrificed two male lambs without blemish and one ewe lamb and a mixture of flour and oil. Pronouncing him "clean," the priest would touch him on the tip of the right ear, the right thumb, and the right big toe with blood and oil. He was then given a certificate declaring him restored.

Such a ceremony would doubtlessly draw a great deal of attention, so despite Jesus' admonition, "Don't tell anyone," the word was going to get out.

Healings today should be confirmed by proper authorities—either spiritual authorities or medical people.

Testimony is needed that the God of miracles is still touching people and healing them.

> Lord, make me like Jesus who reached out and touched the hopeless. Fill me with His Holy Spirit that I, too, may bring healing to the sick. Amen!

EIGHT

ENOUGH FOR EVERYONE
Jesus Feeds 5,000 People with Five Loaves and Two Fish

"There is a lad here . . ."

JOHN 6:1-14
(Also Matthew 14:15-21; Mark 6:30-44; Luke 9:10-17)

Some time after this, Jesus crossed to the far shore of the Sea of Galilee (that is, the Sea of Tiberias), and a great crowd of people followed Him because they saw the miraculous signs He had performed on the sick. Then Jesus went up on the hillside and sat down with His disciples. The Jewish Passover feast was near.

When Jesus looked up and saw a great crowd coming toward Him, He said to Philip, "Where shall we buy bread for these people to eat?" He asked this only to test him, for He already had in mind what He was going to do.

Philip answered Him, "Eight months' wages would not buy enough bread for each one to have a bite!"

Another of His disciples, Andrew, Simon Peter's brother, spoke up, "Here is a boy with five small barley loaves and two small fish, but how far will they go among so many?"

Jesus said, "Have the people sit down." There was plenty of grass in that place, and the men sat down, about five thousand of them. Jesus then took the loaves, gave thanks, and distributed to those who were seated as much as they wanted. He did the same with the fish.

When they had all had enough to eat, He said to
His disciples, "Gather the pieces that are left over. Let
nothing be wasted." So they gathered them and filled
twelve baskets with the pieces of the five barley loaves
left over by those who had eaten.

After the people saw the miraculous sign that Jesus
did, they began to say, "Surely this is the Prophet who
is to come into the world."

I believe the majesty and power of God's miracles is
not just for yesterday; it is for today. That power still exists.
It is God's will and intent that we see His power in miracles.

I believe in miracles.

This earth, the planetary system, and perhaps the entire
universe run on physical laws. The earth tilts on its axis,
turns at a predetermined speed, and rotates around the
sun. That is one of the laws of space which operates without
variation. There are countless other physical laws of
nature—laws of chemistry, laws of mathematics, scientific
laws—that cause our world to be a world of order rather
than a world of chaos. God did not toss this planet into
motion like a frisbee that goes any direction the wind
blows. The world works on the basis of certain absolute
principles and laws. Therefore, even though we may have
limited or no control over the outcome of certain things,
these things can be predicted. Hurricanes, earthquakes,
volcanic eruptions, floods, certain diseases, famines—all
are predictable.

Gradually, as man has learned more about the physical
laws of this universe, he has been able to make these laws
work to his advantage. We have been able to put people
into space where they have discovered new concepts of
these laws. Others work under the sea, researching and
developing. We've been able to look into the brain, replace
damaged organs, expand principles of agriculture, and

develop new methods of transportation, communication, and learning. It's an exciting world in which to live.

However, the discovery of these physical laws is nothing more than the discovery of something God put into motion at the beginning. The whole world was created by God. God put the physical laws there, and we operate by those physical laws. Recognizing the fact that the earth runs by physical law is not humanism, it is pure theism—the recognition of a Higher Power who creates and rules.

Since this is an imperfect universe, damaged by sin, there are exceptions to the laws, of course. Last year, medical doctors revealed they had treated a man in New England whose internal organs were reversed. His heart was on his right side rather than the left. His liver was on his left side, rather than the right. He carried a little tag around his neck saying that all his organs were reversed; that way, if he was in an accident, the doctor would know where to cut on him. There are always exceptions, but basically this world runs on consistent, absolute laws. All things are in God's hands. He is functioning and operating—usually inside His physical laws, but on occasion superseding them for His own glory.

Thus, when Moses and his band of fearful Israelites stood at the edge of the sea and Moses held out his staff, it was God who caused the wind to blow back the waters. When Paul suffered an attack by a poisonous snake, it was God who kept the fatal venom from having its normal effect.

These are things God did long ago—all recorded in the Bible. But miracles are still happening. God, working through His resurrected Son in what Paul calls "the body of Christ" (the church), still causes miracles to take place.

This chapter deals with a wonderful miracle that occurred 2000 years ago at the north end of the Sea of

Galilee where Jesus took five small barley loaves and two small, pickled fish, and fed 5,000 people. Before we look at that miracle, however, let me tell you about an almost identical miracle that took place in 1972.

The story begins in 1964 when a Jesuit priest, Fr. Rick Thomas, was appointed director of Our Lady's Youth Center in El Paso, Texas. Fr. Thomas worked mainly with Hispanics, both in El Paso and across the border in Juarez, Mexico.

In December, 1972, during one of the Bible studies at Our Lady's Youth Center, Fr. Thomas came across a passage in Luke. Jesus said: "When you give a luncheon or a dinner, do not invite your friends, your brothers or relatives, or your rich neighbors; if you do, they may invite you back and so you will be repaid. But when you give a banquet, invite the poor, the crippled, the lame, the blind, and you will be blessed; although they cannot repay you, you will be repaid at the resurrection of the righteous" (Luke 14:12-14).

The words cut like a knife into the priest's heart as he asked himself if he had ever done this. It was embarrassing to admit to himself and the others present that he had lived 44 years and had never been literally obedient to this simple command of Jesus. Many times he had given food to the poor, but he had never thrown a party for them like Jesus wanted.

After mulling this over for several days, Fr. Thomas finally announced to his friends at the prayer meeting that he was going to have Christmas dinner at the garbage dump in Juarez, Mexico. His guests would be the people who lived at the dump—those who made their living as scavengers, picking food out of the garbage to stay alive. He invited his Christian friends from the center to join him.

He scheduled the party for 11 o'clock on Christmas

morning. He asked his Christian friends—those willing to come—to bring something for themselves to eat and something to share with the poor.

Early on Christmas morning, five carloads of people appeared at the center. They set out with 120 burritos— a round Mexican sandwich—some tamales, a ham, chocolate milk, and some fruit, enough food to feed 120 people (if no one ate very much). They drove across the Rio Grande into Mexico. The weather was beautiful—a bright sunny day. In Juarez they were joined by two more cars of Mexican citizens. Then they headed south to the city dump.

Fr. Thomas was filled with apprehension. What would the people at the dump think? What was his group going to do when they got there? The people didn't even know they were coming.

Getting out of the car, he was surprised to learn that the ragpickers didn't even know it was Christmas Day. Furthermore, he discovered the leaders, like union bosses, had divided the dump into two sections. One group lived and worked on one part of the huge dump, the other group lived and worked on the other part. One faction could not walk on the territory of the other. Neither group spoke to the other. Sometimes there were fights, even killings. Yet Jesus wanted Fr. Thomas to invite all of these people to His banquet!

The small group of Christians began to pray, asking God to show them what to do. Finally, after half an hour of negotiation with the leaders, a neutral spot on the east side of the dump was agreed upon. Still separated into hostile camps, the people gathered on either side of a large table where the food was placed.

Fr. Thomas told them his group had come to be with them on Christmas Day—the day Jesus was born. He told them they were going to sing His praises for a while. Then if anyone was sick they would pray for healing, because Jesus liked to heal people. As they sang the people softened, forgetting their barriers. A large number came forward to kneel on the garbage, asking the Christians to lay hands on them for healing.

A significant point was made as they got ready to serve dinner. The priest told the people they were not bringing Christmas baskets to the poor—they had come to share their dinner with them. However, he was not prepared for the number of people who showed up. Most of the garbage pickers, hearing the singing and learning food was available, had stopped their work and come to the tables. More than 300 people were present.

Dismayed at the large number, Fr. Thomas had to tell them they did not have enough for everyone. Then someone suggested: "Let the children eat first." That seemed right, so they bowed for prayer while Fr. Thomas asked God to bless what they had brought.

Knowing they were going to run out of food, Fr. Thomas decided not to eat. Instead, he walked around the edge of the crowd to take some photos. Moments later he noticed children walking through the crowd with brown paper sacks full of food. When Luis, a 20-year-old man, came by, he offered Fr. Thomas a huge piece of the one ham they had brought.

"No, Luis," the priest said, "there is not enough to go around."

"There is more than enough," the Mexican grinned.

"There can't be," Fr. Thomas replied. But as he looked around, he noticed many people had ham in their hands—slices as thick as their hands themselves. How could this be?

When the meal was over, the people went back to work sorting through the garbage. One of the ragpickers invited Fr. Thomas to see where she lived. They walked together on a path through the never-ending piles of charred cans. Finally, she stopped. "This is it!"

"Where?" the priest asked. He saw nothing but a raggedy bedspread laid across the garbage.

"Right here," she said, pointing to the tattered cloth. Only then did he realize he was looking at her home. She slept on the tin cans, wrapped up in the tattered old spread.

As he visited other "homes," he was gripped by the desperateness of it all. He had been to the dump on prior occasions, but his heart was almost broken this time. These were not just beggars—they were his brothers and sisters.

When he returned to the table, he noticed a lot of food packed in the cars of those who had come with him. Inquiring, the Christians just shrugged their shoulders. "It was incredible," one said. "We just kept slicing the ham and it stayed the same size. We handed out the burritos, and when we finished and everyone was full, we had this much left over." In fact, there was so much left over the group was able to stop at three different orphanages on the way home to feed the children.

Fr. Thomas estimates they had brought enough to feed 120; almost 300 had shown up for dinner. All ate their fill and many took bags of groceries away with them. And there was still more than enough.

What had happened? Fr. Thomas says, "Jesus had come to our banquet and multiplied the food—not loaves and fishes as before, but burritos and tamales and ham."

The lesson they learned that day was the lesson we all need to learn as we expect miracles: When God gives an order and men respond, God supplies.

Since then God has continued to supply. Over the years since 1972, Fr. Thomas has prepared hundreds of thousands of meals through his expanding ministry to the poor. He has taught the people to grow their own food, but more important he has taught them to depend on God—who supplies all things.

The miracle at the dump in Juarez, of course, has precedent. It is a repeat of the miracle Jesus performed at a place now called Tabgha, located about two miles southwest of Capernaum, overlooking the Sea of Galilee. There on a large table rock, which is now the altar of the ancient Church of the Multiplication, Jesus performed a miracle of provision that was so astounding it was the only miracle recorded in all four Gospel accounts.

The Arabic name, Tabgha, is derived from the Greek "heptapegon," meaning "seven springs," the source of water for this lovely coastal plain. It was here Jesus came, late one afternoon, to teach.

> *Some time after this, Jesus crossed to the far shore of the Sea of Galilee (that is, the Sea of Tiberias), and a great crowd of people followed Him because they saw the miraculous signs He had performed on the sick. Then Jesus went up on the hillside and sat down with His disciples. The Jewish Passover feast was near.*

Since this was the time of the Passover feast, great crowds of pilgrims from the north would have been moving south toward Jerusalem. Most were walking, of course, with a few riding donkeys. The pilgrimage would take about three weeks—a week to travel, another week to celebrate the feast in Jerusalem, and a final week to return. Many Galilean pilgrims traveling to Jerusalem would cross the Jordan River at the fords near the village of Bethsaida Julias, just north of the Sea of Galilee. They would then skirt the lake on the east side, traveling south through the region of Peraea, and re-cross the Jordan near Jericho. This route was longer, but it avoided the territory of the hated and dangerous Samaritans who lived along the west bank of the Jordan and west to a line that extended from Nazareth almost to Jerusalem.

Word had just reached Jesus of the execution of John the Baptist by King Herod. In those days the only way news could travel was by word of mouth. Newspapers, television, and radio did not exist. It could take up to a year for news from Jerusalem to reach the small villages, while news from Rome might have taken even longer. However, news such as the execution of the nation's foremost prophet would have traveled fast. Since John was Jesus' cousin, runners from Jericho had doubtlessly brought the news within a day's time.

It was a critical time in the life of Jesus. He knew there would be a violent reaction on the part of the people, for despite John's unique lifestyle, he had many followers. His preaching, while radical, was popular. He had denounced the religious leaders as a brood of vipers— which endeared him to those who had suffered under their legalism. His attack on Herod Antipas, denouncing his marriage to Herodias as illicit, enraged the king, who had him imprisoned in the 100-year-old Peraean fortress of Machaerus east of the Dead Sea. It was here he was beheaded at the whim of Herod's vengeful wife.

Jesus expected two things to happen. He expected the people to react against John's execution, which would bring swift reprisals from the Roman overlords. Knowing of Jesus' relationship to John, the Romans would probably blame Him as one of the insurrectionists. It would be a good idea to withdraw until the clamor died down.

Jesus also knew the crowds, hearing of John's death, would turn to Him. Looking for a deliverer, they would try to cast Him in the role of a militant Messiah, for the nation was on the brink of revolution against the Romans. In fact, within eyesight of Capernaum was Mount Arbel, towering over the western shore of the Sea of Galilee above Tiberias. On the northern cliffs of the mountain, visible from below but virtually inaccessible, were the fascinating cave fortresses of a militant group called the Zealots. In fact, one of Jesus' disciples, Simon the Zealot, had belonged to this group of highly militant Jews. After the fall of Jerusalem, the Zealots made a final, futile stand against the Romans at a lonely mountain fortress in the Negev Desert called Masada. All died.

Knowing the spirit of the Zealots was strong in the Galilean area, Jesus felt it wise to withdraw when He received the news of John's execution. He had not come as a military deliverer, as the Jews believed the Messiah would be, but as a suffering servant.

A week or so earlier, Jesus had sent out His 12 disciples on a preaching and healing mission. They had returned, filled with enthusiasm, and reported to Jesus the results of their mission. Jesus had been teaching in Capernaum, and when He finished it was late afternoon. He and His disciples got in a couple of fishing boats and set sail around the coast about four miles to the little town of Bethsaida—hoping to be alone. But the people had been watching with astonishment the things Jesus had been doing, and rushed along the shoreline to the place where the Jordan River flows into the lake from the north. Expecting Jesus to head for the fords of the Jordan at Bethsaida Julius, they raced toward the little village—many of them actually arriving before Jesus did.

Galilee was a hard place in which to get alone. A small section of the nation, it was only 50 miles from north to south and 25 miles from east to west. At the time of Jesus, according to the Jewish historian Josephus, there were 204 towns and villages in that small area, none with a population of less than 15,000. It was one of the most thickly populated regions on earth at that time.

It must have been frustrating to Jesus never to find the time He needed to be alone. He was under continuous strain, and this time, in particular, He needed to escape from the crowds to avoid a head-on collision with Herod or the Roman troops. Yet at the sight of the crowds, Jesus' sympathy was kindled. They were hungry for God and He responded to that hunger by wanting to feed them. "Man does not live on bread alone," He had admonished Satan when the devil had tempted Him to turn rocks into bread, "but on every word that comes from the mouth of God."

He had been feeding these spiritually hungry people God's bread. But Jesus knew that physical hunger is just as real as spiritual hunger. Seeing the huge crowd, which numbered 5,000 men alone (not to mention the women and children which could have swelled the mob to as many as 15,000), Jesus did an astonishing thing. He turned to His disciples and ordered them to feed the multitude.

> When Jesus looked up and saw a great crowd coming toward Him, He said to Philip, "Where shall we buy bread for these people to eat?"

Matthew says, "When Jesus landed and saw a large crowd, He had compassion on them and healed their sick" (Matthew 14:14). Writing primarily to Jews who had little or no compassion, Matthew consistently emphasized the compassion of Jesus. Jesus, he pointed out, never dealt with people according to His need, but according to theirs. Others always came first in the life and ministry of Jesus.

The recounting of the miracle stories is different in each Gospel. The biographers—Matthew, Mark, Luke, and John—wrote the life of Jesus from their own perspective. Matthew, quite Jewish, loved writing of the Old Testament prophecies which Jesus fulfilled. Mark, a young militant, filled his Gospel with action stories. Luke, a physician, was a storyteller. John, writing from recollection in his old age, is much more philosophical. Thus, when Jesus asks Philip, "Where shall we buy bread for these people to eat?" John adds: "He asked this only to test him, for He already had in mind what He was going to do."

Why did He turn to Philip, one of His twelve disciples? Philip, like Andrew and Peter, was from nearby Bethsaida. He came from this area. Since they were near his hometown, it would be natural for Jesus to turn and ask Philip, "Where is the local grocery store? Is there a 7-Eleven close by? I haven't been into this area very often; do you know of a place where we can buy food?"

Jesus was having a good time with Philip, kidding him. Philip's answer is serious, however. Looking out over the huge mob of people who filled the grassy basin which extended toward the north shore of the lake, he answered, despairing, "Eight months' wages would not buy enough bread for each one to have a bite!"

Philip was a practical man. Had he been part of the 20th century, he would probably have had a degree in engineering. He quickly calculated a few things in his mind and said, "Five thousand people! We can't feed 5,000 people by natural laws. Anyway, they're not our responsibility. If they were foolish enough to get out here on the road without food, let them suffer a little bit. Pretty soon they will learn to get it like we do." Obviously, Philip was rather negative about the whole situation—which was probably the reason Jesus was jesting with him.

One would think that when Jesus had exhausted Himself by teaching and healing, and sensing His own need to withdraw from the crowd for safety's sake, He would have felt He had done all He could for these people. After all, He hadn't asked them to follow Him. In fact, He had tried to escape the crowds. They knew it was near sundown, that this was a desolate section and there was no food available. Each man should fend for himself. That is the way the natural mind works. Jesus, though, saw people with the eyes of God. It was time for a miracle.

> *Another of His disciples, Andrew, Simon Peter's brother, spoke up, "Here is a boy with five small barley loaves and two small fish, but how far will they go among so many?"*

Andrew, also a native of Bethsaida, seems to have overheard Jesus' question to Philip. He stepped forward with a small boy in tow. The boy, Andrew had discovered, had five barley loaves and two little fishes. Barley was the cheapest of all bread and was held in contempt. It was the bread of the poor. The fishes would have been no bigger than sardines. In those days, fresh fish was an unheard of luxury, for there was no means of refrigerating it, transporting it any distance, and keeping it edible. The small, sardine-like fish which swarmed the waters of the Sea of Galilee were caught and pickled so they could be stored for later eating. Assuming the boy was from Bethsaida and known to Andrew, this would have been part of the picnic lunch his mother had prepared when the family joined the crowd who came out to see the miracle-worker.

Andrew was naturally doubtful. His faith was small. But when the little boy came to him, offering to share his scant meal with the multitude, he knew he had no choice but to offer it to Jesus. It was all Jesus needed.

While Philip had no faith at all, Andrew's wasn't much larger—no bigger than a mustard seed. But all Jesus ever expects is mustard-seed faith.

It's at this point John gives us insight into the heart of God. Seeing the little boy standing there with his tiny lunch, Jesus did not hesitate. "Have the people sit down," He commanded.

All it takes is somebody who is willing to say, "I'll take a tiny step toward the impossible." Take that step and immediately God says, "I will multiply your tiny step a billion times." All it takes is faith the size of a grain of mustard seed. Plant it in God's fertile soil and it will grow up into a huge tree so big that even birds can come and make their nests in it.

The little boy's action illustrates a basic spiritual principle: If you will take what little bit you have and offer it to God, God will do the multiplication. Maybe all you can say is: "Lord, I don't believe, but I want to." Even the admission is a faith statement. At least you are saying, "God, You can. . . ."

That's what Andrew and his little sidekick did—they offered what they had to Jesus.

> Jesus said, "Have the people sit down." There was plenty of grass in that place, and the men sat down, about five thousand of them. Jesus then took the loaves, gave thanks, and distributed to those who were seated as much as they wanted. He did the same with the fish.

Jesus was acting as the father of the family as He commanded the people to sit down and then blessed them. The Jewish grace He used would be the one that was used in every home: "Blessed art Thou, Jehovah our God, King of the universe, Who causes to come forth bread from the earth." It was a blessing all Jews repeated over every morsel—but this time it had genuine meaning. God was about to cause bread to come forth from the earth, not through wheat and barley grain, but through a miracle of instant creation.

When they had all had enough to eat, He said to His disciples,
"Gather the pieces that are left over. Let nothing be wasted."

What happened here? I have heard all kinds of
explanations. Nobody really knows. How did the miracle
of multiplication take place? Did it take place in the
blessing—as Jesus blessed the loaves, did they just get
bigger and bigger? Did it take place in the distribution—
as the disciples took the five loaves and went out to
distribute them, did more bread simply appear in their
hands? Did it take place in the eating? When did the miracle
take place? Even though this is the only miracle story
recounted by all four biographers, not a single word is
said about the actual method of the miracle. In fact, it
seems to be a deliberate omission, as if the Holy Spirit
forbade the writers to recount it—a phenomena which
occurs with all the other miracles as well. Some things
are hidden, not just to keep us from trying to imitate them,
or to prevent us from making a sacred formula out of
them, but because they are incomprehensible. They
remain, and ever will be, mysteries. The real impact of
this passage is not in the mechanics of the miracle. The
real impact is in what caused it to take place to start with—
a couple of hearts turned toward God. Jesus believed, of
course. (He already knew what was going to happen.) Then
there was a little kid who brought his meal and said, "Take
mine." He gave everything. And there was a disciple who
said, "It's not very much, but maybe we can do a little
bit with it." God looked upon all those things, and the
miracle of multiplication took place. Enough for everyone.

One twentieth-century Bible commentator has an
interesting theory about the feeding of the 5,000. He
suggests that the miracle was not in the multiplication of
the food, but in the spirit of unselfishness which swept

through the crowd when they saw the little boy offer up his meager lunch.

Artists of the Middle Ages are responsible for many of our biblical concepts. Most of those artists, however, knew little of the customs of Jesus' day. For instance, while the Jews were a wandering people, they had no suitcases. Instead they carried with them a *kophinos*, a wicker basket shaped like a narrow-necked pitcher, broadening out at the base. Both ends were attached to a cord so it could be slung over a shoulder. Ancient Roman historians often wrote of "the Jew with his basket and his truss of hay." (The truss of hay was used as a bed, and was often referred to as a "mat" or "bed.") The basket *(kophinos)* was a part of his life. He carried it partly because many Jews were accomplished beggars, and into the basket went the results of his begging. Also, the orthodox Jew used it to tote his own food supplies, so that he would be certain of eating food that was ceremonially clean and pure.

Thus, these pilgrims on their way to Jerusalem for the feast of Passover would have certainly had food with them, stashed away in their baskets. But they were stingy, afraid to share for fear they would use up all their food before the end of the trip. But when they saw the generosity of a small boy, it pricked their hearts. When Jesus blessed the five loaves and started passing them out, they reached into their baskets and brought out their own loaves— sharing them, also.

That's a very beautiful story. Maybe it happened that way. God is capable, of course, of making stingy people generous. But I suspect had it really happened that way, at least one of the four biographers would have mentioned it. Instead, all leave the impression it was a genuine miracle of multiplication—even greater than the one which took place on the garbage dump in Juarez, Mexico, 2000 years later. It was a miracle of provision.

We are dealing with a God of miracles, who loves to intervene in people's lives, who loves to change the course of physical action. Many times all He is waiting for is somebody who will say, "Here's my lunch, Jesus, do with it what You will."

> *When they had all had enough to eat, He said to His disciples, "Gather the pieces that are left over. Let nothing be wasted." So they gathered them and filled twelve baskets with the pieces of the five barley loaves left over by those who had eaten.*

Where did the baskets come from? The Jew and his basket! Each of the 12 disciples had his own.

> *After the people saw the miraculous sign that Jesus did, they began to say, "Surely this is the Prophet who is to come into the world." Jesus, knowing that they intended to come and make Him king by force, withdrew again into the hills by Himself.*

Unlike men, Jesus did not want applause. He fed the people because He loved them, because He had compassion on them. He performed His miracle to show practical-minded Philip and the other disciples that God is not limited to engineering principles, that He doesn't always follow the rules of the financial planner, and that He sometimes blesses foolish people. The same God who turned water into wine when the host miscalculated also fed 5,000 people who foolishly got trapped away from home without any food.

Jesus exhibits this principle here. "I did it because I loved them, that was all," Jesus responded to His disciples when the miraculous meal was over. "Now, let's get out of here before they try to make Me king."

God loves those who help people and then don't hang around to get the credit.

Several years ago I flew from my home on the east coast of Florida to Norfolk, Virginia, where I was to host the popular Christian television show, The 700 Club. My plane was delayed in Atlanta and I called ahead to Jackie Mitchum, the show's guest coordinator, telling her I would not arrive until 2:00 a.m. I urged her to call the studio's driver, who was waiting for me at the airport, and have him go home and go to bed. I would catch a cab to the hotel. She agreed, and said the driver would pick me up at the hotel the next morning and take me to the studio.

It was snowing and icy when I arrived at the Norfolk airport. There was one lone taxi sitting out front in the snow. The driver was asleep in the front seat. I climbed in, woke the driver and told him I wanted to go to the Omni Hotel in downtown Norfolk. As we drove, I tried to engage the sleepy man in conversation. He was unresponsive, so I settled back in the seat as we moved through the almost deserted streets. For some reason, however, I couldn't get my attention off the cab driver. All I could see was the back of his head in the darkened car. I prayed, silently, "Lord, is there something I'm supposed to do?"

Instantly, I sensed something in my heart, almost as if a voice were speaking. "I want you to bless the cab driver," God seemed to be saying. "He has some big needs."

"Lord, is that the reason you delayed the plane and had me arrive at 2:00 a.m. in a snowstorm?"

"Just bless him for Me," the answer came.

Once again I tried to get the man to talk. All he did was mumble some response.

"How can I bless him if he won't listen to me?" I asked.

"When a man is hurting you need to speak his language,"

God seemed to be saying.

Then we were at the hotel.

"How much do I owe you?" I asked, thinking I had missed my chance to bless him.

"Seven dollars," the driver mumbled. Then he added, "It's hard to feed a family on a night like tonight."

Suddenly I knew how I was supposed to bless him.

I handed him a $10 bill and told him to keep the change. He looked up and smiled. Then I handed him a $20 bill. "What's that for?" he asked, looking suspicious.

"God wants to bless you," I said. "He sent me along to deliver this to you so you will know how much He loves you."

I picked up my suitcase, closed the door, and ran through the snow to the hotel. Inside, watching the cab slowly pull away from the curb, I felt warm and good. He didn't know my name—but he knew my business. I was a representative of God. That was all that mattered. I had planted a seed. Some place down the line, someone else will water the seed. Another will fertilize. And someday, someone will harvest the crop and call it a miracle.

All that is required for a miracle is someone who is willing to listen, obey—and get out of the way.

> Use me, Lord, to feed those who hunger and thirst for righteousness, as well as those who merely hunger and thirst. For Jesus' sake and their sake. Amen.

NINE

POWER TO CAST OUT EVIL SPIRITS
A Confrontation in the Valley

"Everything is possible for him who believes."

MARK 9:14-29
(also Matthew 17:14-21 and Luke 9:37-43)

When they came to the other disciples, they saw a large crowd around them and the teachers of the law arguing with them. As soon as all the people saw Jesus, they were overwhelmed with wonder and ran to greet Him.

"What are you arguing with them about?" He asked.

A man in the crowd answered, "Teacher, I brought You my son, who is possessed by a spirit that has robbed him of speech. Whenever it seizes him, it throws him to the ground. He foams at the mouth, gnashes his teeth and becomes rigid. I asked Your disciples to drive out the spirit but they could not."

"O unbelieving generation," Jesus replied, "how long shall I stay with you? How long shall I put up with you? Bring the boy to Me."

So they brought him. When the spirit saw Jesus, it immediately threw the boy into a convulsion. He fell to the ground and rolled around, foaming at the mouth.

181

Jesus asked the boy's father, "How long has he been like this?"

"From childhood," he answered, "It has often thrown him into fire or water to kill him. But if You can do anything, take pity on us and help us."

"If you can?" said Jesus. "Everything is possible for him who believes."

Immediately the boy's father exclaimed, "I do believe; help me overcome my unbelief."

When Jesus saw that a crowd was running to the scene, He rebuked the evil spirit. "You deaf and dumb spirit," He said, "I command you, come out of him and never enter him again."

The spirit shrieked, convulsed him violently and came out. The boy looked so much like a corpse that many said, "He's dead." But Jesus took him by the hand and lifted him to his feet, and he stood up.

After Jesus had gone indoors, His disciples asked Him privately, "Why couldn't we drive it out?"

He replied, "This kind can come out only by prayer [and fasting]."

The Gospels we find in the New Testament—four of them: Matthew, Mark, Luke, and John—are all biographies of the life of Jesus, each written from a different perspective.

John, who was the philosopher, was really writing much, much later than any of the rest of them, perhaps as much as 50 years following the death of Jesus. He writes from a very loving and philosophical viewpoint, different from the other biographers.

Matthew, Mark, and Luke probably used a common source for their material, aside from their own personal relationship with Jesus. Bible scholars seem to think— and I agree—that there was probably some other written source which has been lost across the years from which they all drew. Perhaps these were words written by Simon Peter. As a result these synoptic Gospels have many similarities. Some of the stories are identical.

One of the stories which appears in all three of the synoptic Gospels is the story of the miracle Jesus performed on His return from His trip up Mount Hermon—the Mount of Transfiguration. The story is similar in its foundation, but there are some significant differences as each one of the Gospel writers remembers something else about that event. Whether they were all there when this took place, we're not sure. We do know that none of the biographers were with Jesus on Mount Hermon. Only Peter, James, and John accompanied Him on that occasion. However, if Peter did make notes, then it stands to reason the biographers used them when writing their versions. However, any or all of them could have been present when Jesus returned and had His encounter with the demon-possessed child.

THE PLACE: The base of Mount Hermon on the Lebanese border in northern Israel. Snow-capped most of the year, Mount Hermon towers 9,101 feet above sea level as an Israeli sentinal between Israel on the south and Lebanon and Syria on the north and east. Its melting snowcap provides the water for the Jordan River, which fills the beautiful blue Sea of Galilee and later empties into the Dead Sea at the lowest spot on the surface of the earth. In his beautiful psalm of unity, David said unity among men was "as if the dew of Hermon were falling on Mount Zion" (Psalm 133:3).

If you visit Israel today, you may be told the Mount of Transfiguration is Mount Tabor, located on the southeast of Nazareth. However, a reading of the Bible clearly indicates it was Mount Hermon which Jesus ascended with His three friends, and it was at the base of Mount Hermon, far to the north of the Sea of Galilee, where this miracle took place.

THE OCCASION: Jesus had just descended from a brief stay on the high slopes of the mountain. Three of His disciples, Peter, James, and John—his "inner circle"—had climbed the mountain with Him. On this Mount of Transfiguration, both Moses and Elijah had appeared, and God had spoken directly to Jesus—as His disciples listened. Peter wanted to stay, but Jesus knew His real ministry was not alone on the mountaintop, but with hurting people in the valley below.

The moment on the mountain was a necessary time in Jesus' life. It was here He received additional revelation concerning His mission on earth. His disciples, however, like so many of us, were caught up in the experience and did not understand that the transfiguration was a means to a greater end, not an end in itself. Peter, enthralled by what he saw, reacted as many of today's Christians act—he wanted to build some kind of monument to commemorate the event. But if the ascent to the mountain was essential to the mission of Jesus, the descent into the valley was even more an imperative.

I remember a special conversation I had with my Jewish guide on one of my visits to Mount Sinai. Anwar Sadat, then president of Egypt, had just proposed that Jews, Christians, and Moslems cooperate by building three monuments on top of Mount Sinai, since all three faiths look back to that place as sacred to their history. A number of American Christians had responded—excited over the concept.

"Let the Christians and Moslems build their monuments," the Jewish zealot had snorted. "Monuments are for the dead. We Jews serve a living God."

It was a fitting and proper rebuke.

Peter not only wanted to build monuments on Mount Hermon, he wanted to remain right there—basking in the memory of what had taken place. All of us have our sacred places, and our sacred memories—memories we'd like to prolong indefinitely. But the purpose of mountaintops is to prepare us for the valleys—the battles and routines of life. There is a place for the dreamer, but dreamers never accomplish anything unless they wake up and go to work.

It was said of the great explorer, Captain Scott, that he was "a strange mixture of the dreamy and the practical and never more practical than immediately after he had been dreamy." We cannot live without our dreams and memories, but we cannot live in them either.

The essence of life demands confrontation with problems—and problem people. A friend once told me, when asked what ministry he wanted to pursue, that his ideal was to be a research librarian in the world's greatest theological library—where no people were allowed to enter. Solitude is a necessary part of our Christian experience—but this must never lead to solitariness. Every prisoner knows the dread of solitary confinement. It's one thing to be private, another thing to be entirely separated from people. Solitude is necessary if a man is to keep his contact with God, but if a man, in his search for essential solitude, shuts himself away from people, if he closes his ears to the cries for help, if he feels that his time alone with God is more important than helping God's people, then he has missed God completely. The purpose of solitude is to make us effective when we meet people in ministry.

It was in the valley, at the base of Mount Hermon, that Jesus came face to face with a situation that demanded a miracle—a miracle of deliverance.

One of the revelations Jesus received on Mount Hermon

concerned the rest of His mission on earth. God had spoken to Him, letting Him know that there was no way to fulfill this mission except through death—death on a cross. Jesus was going to die, shortly, at the hands of men. But God was going to resurrect Him.

It seems that Jesus, while on earth, did not have full knowledge of everything that was to happen. When He assumed His earthly form, He gave up the knowledge He had previously enjoyed while in the presence of God. In His earthly form, He was having to listen to God, moment by moment by moment, for additional revelation concerning the future. One of the things He didn't know was the full story of what was going to happen as God brought the whole redemption of the earth to pass. God revealed to Him, bit by bit, that this would include death on the cross, followed by a resurrection. He was living solely by revelation knowledge, listening to His Father and doing only what He told Him to do.

Descending from the mountain, Jesus was now face to face with an impossible situation. This is so typical of life. One day we are having a great experience with the Lord; the next day the bottom falls out of everything. One day we are in the presence of the God of the impossible, coming away with a powerful faith that says, "nothing can stop me now." The next moment we are faced with the impossible—and we are powerless.

> When they came to the other disciples, they saw a large crowd around them and the teachers of the law arguing with them.

A large crowd had gathered where Jesus had left His other disciples. There was a theological debate—a loud one—going on between the disciples and the scribes—the teachers of the law. Jesus must have been exasperated.

POWER TO CAST OUT EVIL SPIRITS 187

He had just been in the presence of His Father, had seen both Moses and Elijah face to face, and now He was in the middle of another one of those endless and meaningless theological arguments which seemed to go on at all hours of the day and night as men tried to explain, or explain away, God.

This time the men were arguing about demons. Are there even such things as demons? Can a godly man be possessed of demons? If he is afflicted with demons, is he oppressed, obsessed, or possessed? What methods should you use to exorcise demons? Can children be possessed by demons?

Jesus never got involved in these arguments. He just cast the demons out and went on His way.

The human tendency would have been to say, "I've got bigger things to do than to settle a stupid religious argument. People have been arguing about these things ever since Moses. I've got more on My mind right now. So don't bother Me. I've just gotten a message from God that I'm going to have to hang on a cross for folks like you, so bug off. Leave Me alone."

Jesus, though, never turned away from genuine human need.

> As soon as all the people saw Jesus, they were overwhelmed with wonder and ran to greet Him. "What are you arguing with them about?" He asked.

"They're arguing over my son," a man in the crowd answered.

"Your son?"

"I had hoped You'd be here," the man answered. "My little boy has an evil spirit. The spirit has stolen his hearing and his speech. Whenever it seizes him, the boy falls to the ground and goes into convulsions. He foams at the mouth, gnashes his teeth, and becomes rigid. When I could not find You I asked Your disciples to drive out the spirit, but they were powerless."

Jesus must have just shaken His head in exasperation. Luke's version of the story makes it even stronger. Here we find the father's language vivid. He told Jesus the demon "dashed him down." It is the word used when a boxer deals a knock-out blow to his opponent.

Luke's version gives additional insight. "I begged Your disciples to drive it [the demon] out, but they could not" (Luke 9:40). The disciples knew it was an evil spirit which was seizing the child and trying to kill him, but they were powerless to drive it out. In order to understand why Jesus felt exasperated, you need to drop back to Luke 9:1 and read the beginning of this entire episode. The story begins when Jesus sent out His twelve disciples with a commission.

> When Jesus had called the Twelve together, He gave them power and authority to drive out all demons and to cure diseases, and He sent them out to preach the kingdom of God and to heal the sick. (Luke 9:1-2)

Power and authority to drive out all demons. Later these same men returned, saying they had had marvelous success. "Why," they gushed, "even the demons are subject to the authority You have given to us." They were riding on a spiritual high. Then, suddenly, they were confronted with something too big to handle.

What had happened? Maybe the secret to their powerlessness lay in the fact the disciples failed to take authority, and instead got into an argument with the religious people about the existence of demons. In fact, Matthew, who was something of a scribe, an expert in Jewish law, indicates the child may have been epileptic. He uses the word *seleniazesthai*, which literally means *to be moonstruck*, to describe the boy's condition.

Or, perhaps the disciples had simply gotten cocky. Jesus was away, and they had started bragging to the scribes of their new power. "Why, we even have the power to cast out demons and heal the sick," they said.

"Uh-huh," the skeptics muttered. Then one of them sneaked away from the conversation and told the father that Jesus' disciples were nearby. Why didn't he bring his demon-possessed son and see if they could set him free? It was a test made to order, and of course, they failed. God always lets you fail when He knows you're going to take credit for it if you succeed.

The sad spectacle gave the scribes just what they were looking for. The helplessness of the disciples was a first-rate opportunity to sneer not just at them, but at their Master. That's what made the situation so tragic. The conduct, the words, the behavior, the inability of God's people to cope with life produces criticism toward God Himself. The opponents of God are ever looking for some reason to prove God isn't worthy to be praised, much less obeyed. These opponents use us as their yardstick, not only to justify their own misbehavior, but to judge God. It does not matter how lofty our preaching or how high our ideals, if we cannot produce a change in our own life, everything we say is of no effect.

Yet in spite of the disciples' failure, the father never doubted the power of Jesus Himself. It was as if he said, "If only I can get to Jesus. He'll know what to do."

It's a problem that exists even today. There are many who have discovered that most of today's Christians, and most of today's churches, are not what they make themselves out to be. They hold out great hopes, they talk about power and authority, but when it comes right down to it, most of them are powerless. Even so, in the deep places of our hearts we know that if we could only get beyond the programs of the church, the money raising schemes of God's people, the big tell-and-no-show of the professional religionist—if we could only get past the human failure and touch Jesus, we'd be healed.

Picture Peter—Peter, who has just been with Jesus on the mountaintop. This was the very kind of thing he wanted to avoid. It was probably Peter who first wrote this story to begin with. He has just come down from the Mount of Transfiguration with Jesus. He has seen things no man has ever seen before. Moses was there, Elijah was there—men who had been dead for more than 1,000 years. He had been in the presence of all the saints in heaven. God had pulled back the drapes and allowed Peter to see directly into Glory. Now this.

Picture Jesus. It's a rare moment of irritation for Jesus. We don't find Jesus irritated many times. He has come down from the mountain where He has just learned that soon He is to accomplish His mission in Jerusalem. He had been literally transfigured, adorned with a heavenly light, caught, the reality of the cross had been revealed. For the first time He realized He was going to have to suffer untold physical agony and pain—not to mention the spiritual agony. Now, when He really needs to be quiet and assimilate all He had just experienced, He's thrust into the middle of a stupid argument and realizes the men He's been training to take over when He leaves are both stupid and powerless. He responds by rebuking, first the mob of scoffers, then His own disciples.

> *O unbelieving generation, how long shall I stay with you? How long shall I put up with you? Bring the boy to Me.*

What do you do in times like these?
You do what you can.

Everybody can do something to help someone. It may not seem like much. Maybe you can't do anything to change the world. Maybe you can't do anything to change your church. Maybe you're stuck in prison—and will continue to be stuck there a long time. Maybe you can't do anything to change your own miserable circumstances. But there's always something you can do—for someone, for something.

I remember one night I was so depressed about the world situation, about events in our church, about the image of God which was being dragged through the slime and mire in the public media. I had prayed, but I felt powerless to change things. It was a low time in my life. I walked out in the backyard with several of my little grandchildren. One of them said to me, "Booger's dying." Booger was my son's puppy, and his little boys were crying. For three days the little dog had been sick. That afternoon he had lost the ability to walk. He wouldn't eat or drink. I walked over to where he was lying on a towel. The little boys had covered him with an old bedsheet. The oldest, T.J., aged six, looked up at me with tears in his eyes.

"PaPa, can't God heal Booger?"

"God can do anything, T.J."

"Will you pray for Booger, PaPa?"

Who was I to pray? I had been praying for all kinds of things and nothing seemed to be working out.

"Please, PaPa."

I knelt down beside the little dog and laid my hands on his quivering body. "Lord, this is about the only thing I have faith for right how. But it's important to these kids that Booger gets well. And I guess it's important to Booger. And it's important to me. . . ."

As I prayed, I felt faith growing in me. In just a moment I was rebuking the sickness and taking authority over anything that would try to kill my possessions and destroy my faith and the faith of my grandchildren. I ended the prayer almost shouting.

"PaPa, is Booger going to get well?"

"You bet, kids. God loves little dogs just as much as you do."

Brash? What if the dog had died, you ask? Wouldn't that have hurt the children's faith in God? But if we hadn't prayed, there would have been no faith to lose. It was worth the risk.

And wouldn't you know—when we came out the next morning, Booger was running around the house, barking at squirrels in the trees.

There is always something that presents itself before you that, if you will do it, then God will do something else. If you will be faithful in the little things, then God will give you power and authority and knowledge in the big things.

As the English poet, Kingsley, once wrote:

> Do the work that's nearest,
> Though it's dull at whiles,
> Helping when you meet them
> Lame dogs over stiles.

Jesus asked the boy's father, "How long has he been like this?"

> *"From childhood," he answered. "It has often thrown him into fire or water to kill him. But if You can do anything, take pity on us and help us."*

The father didn't know Jesus. All he knew were the disciples who had been standing around bragging about the fact they had the power to cast out demons—and couldn't.

"If you can?" Jesus seems to repeat the question. But He's not repeating it. The "you" is not a rhetorical reference back to what the man had just said. Rather, Jesus is talking to the man himself. He says, "If *you*, father of the child, if *you* can." Then He adds, "Everything is possible for him who believes."

Jesus is dealing with a universal truth. He is saying that faith resides in the individual. If you can do it. . . . It's an exciting approach to life. Our problem is our lack of faith. The cure for your boy, Jesus says, depends not on Me, but on you. To approach anything with a spirit of hopelessness makes it hopeless. Any time you say a thing is impossible, it becomes impossible.

To say any disease is incurable makes that disease terminal. Medical authorities say the disease of AIDS is incurable. And it is, on a physical level. But in the realm of miracles, nothing is impossible—even curing AIDS.

All you need, Jesus says, is faith. Faith in what? Faith in healing? Oh, no, that's not it. What we need is faith in God. If you believe in God, then all things are possible. You have now risen above the dimensions of the physical into the realm of the spiritual, where God operates. In that realm all things are possible.

What Christians need—what we all need—is a sense of the possible. Most of us, though, are cursed with a sense of the impossible. All our lives we've been told "no," "don't touch that," "you'll be sorry if you do that." We've been told certain things were for Jesus—and certain things are for us. Jesus could perform miracles because He was perfect, we were told. But us . . . we'll be lucky if we barely squeeze into heaven. Whenever we are faced with a difficult situation, we respond by thinking "Uh-oh, this one is bigger than I am. This one is impossible. I can handle the little ones, but this one is impossible." That is precisely why miracles do not happen.

So the father can only say, "Help me if You can." Then he is face to face with Jesus, and a miraculous thing happens. Suddenly something blazes up inside the father. "I believe!" he exclaims. It's a kind of a "Wow! I believe!" Then he adds, "Help me overcome my unbelief."

In other words, I don't even want to go back to where I was. Close that thing off. Seal it. I don't ever want to drop back down to the old level of seeing things from the natural. From now on, I want to remain where I am right now—seeing things from the supernatural.

He is saying, in essence, the same thing Peter said on the Mount of Transfiguration. I don't ever want to go back into the valley. I want to remain forever on the mountaintop of faith. Only this time, the request is legitimate—for he's not talking about building an earthly tabernacle, he's telling Jesus he wants to remain in the tabernacle of God. And that's where He wants all of us to be.

Do you see what Jesus did? He walked down into the valley, grabbed hold of this man's spirit, and put him up on the Mount of Transfiguration, where they had all been just before. Then He says, "Even though you live in the valley, your spirit can live on the mountaintop." The man grabbed hold of that and said, "Hallelujah! I don't ever want to go back down there again."

It was then Jesus rebuked the evil spirit.

"You deaf and dumb spirit," He said, "I command you, come out of him and never enter him again."

He calls the spirit by name. He knew what it was. Matthew suggests the boy had epilepsy. Epilepsy, of course, is a legitimate disease that is caused by problems with the electrical impulses in the brain. That's not to say all epilepsy is caused by demons. But anytime you see a situation where there is a weakness in the human body, you will find Satan attacking that particular weakness by sending his demons to try to take over. In the case of this boy, they had been successful.

Does that mean demons are responsible for every sickness, every impossible situation? Of course not. Most of the people Jesus healed were not afflicted by demons. However, the wise Christian knows he should ever be on the lookout for demonic presence—even when ministering to children. That's awesome, to think that a child can be possessed by a demon. However, we find at least two other occurrences in the Scriptures where they brought children to Jesus who were demon-possessed. In each of these instances, Jesus dealt with them and cast the demons out.

Here He does the same thing. He speaks to the demon, and there is a physical manifestation. Demons seldom leave a person peacefully. They hate to leave and often tear and rip a person as they are forced to leave under the authority of Jesus. But leave they must when a believer takes authority over them. The Bible says: "The word of God is nigh upon thee, even in thy mouth." *The name of Jesus in the mouth of a believer is the most powerful force in the world.*

It was total and complete deliverance. In this case the boy's illness was caused by a demon. By removing the demon from the situation, the illness cured itself.

Jesus didn't come just to save us from our sin so we can get to heaven. He came that we could have life abundant here on earth at the same time. Well, you can't have abundant life if a demon is throwing you into the fire. That's not very abundant. That's a tortured life. But Jesus says to us what He said to His disciples: "I have given you power and authority to drive out all demons and to cure diseases."

Why, the disciples asked Jesus when they got Him alone, were we powerless, while You were able to set the boy free with just a word?

Jesus gave a very interesting answer:

"This kind can come out only by prayer."

Some of the older manuscripts use the phrase, "prayer and fasting." What was Jesus saying? For one thing, He was saying there are ranks of demons. He seems to be distinguishing between this one and others less powerful. There are some demons that come out easily and some that don't. This one was a tenacious demon. He was thoroughly rooted. To drive him out, one would need a different approach than the one used by the disciples. Remember, they had, in the past, been successful in casting out demons.

So Jesus says this kind can come out only through prayer, or prayer and fasting. What was He talking about? Jesus didn't stop to pray or to fast. He didn't say, "Wait here, I'll be back in three days after I've fasted and prayed." He just spoke the word and the demon left.

But, in fact, Jesus had just come down from the mountain where He had been praying and fasting. He had not been praying and fasting for this little boy. He didn't even know the child was down there, waiting for Him. But Jesus lived a "fasted life." He was not only prepared to give up food, He was prepared to give up His very life. He lived a cross-life, a life of constant sacrifice. No demon can withstand that kind of life. No wonder when He spoke, the demon had to leave.

So Jesus says to His disciples, "You don't live close enough to God. If you lived close enough to God, you would be equipped with power." God gives us gifts, but they are useless unless we use them for Him.

There is a profound lesson here: What we do in private, in our relationship with God, is more important than what we do in public. If we do things in private in our relationship with God, He will use us in public ministry elsewhere. All He requires is that we remain close to Him.

Lord, I'm grateful for the revelation that power is still given to Your people, that we have authority over the underworld. I'm grateful we have authority to heal the sick, to perform miracles—all in the name of Jesus. More important, Lord, I pray You will invigorate us with the desire to know You in a deeper way, so Your glory may be manifested out across this earth through us. In Jesus' name, Amen.

Ten

Power Over Death
Jesus Raises Lazarus from the Dead

"I am the resurrection and the life. He who believes in Me will live, even though he dies. . . ."

JOHN 11:17-44

On His arrival, Jesus found that Lazarus had already been in the tomb for four days. Bethany was less than two miles from Jerusalem, and many Jews had come to Martha and Mary to comfort them in the loss of their brother. When Martha heard that Jesus was coming, she went out to meet Him, but Mary stayed at home.

"Lord," Martha said to Jesus, "If You had been here, my brother would not have died. But I know that even now God will give You whatever You ask."

Jesus said to her, "Your brother will rise again."

Martha answered, "I know he will rise again in the resurrection at the last day."

Jesus said to her, "I am the resurrection and the life. He who believes in Me will live, even though he dies; and whoever lives and believes in Me will never die. Do you believe this?"

"Yes, Lord," she told Him, "I believe that You are the Christ, the Son of God, who was to come into the world."

And after she had said this, she went back and called her sister Mary aside. "The Teacher is here," she said, "and is asking for you." When Mary heard this, she got up quickly and went to Him. Now Jesus had not yet entered the village, but was still at the place where Martha had met Him. When the Jews who had been with Mary in the house, comforting her, noticed how quickly she got up and went out, they followed her, supposing she was going to the tomb to mourn there.

When Mary reached the place where Jesus was and saw Him, she fell at His feet and said, "Lord, if You had been here, my brother would not have died."

When Jesus saw her weeping, and the Jews who had come along with her also weeping, He was deeply moved in spirit and troubled. "Where have you laid him?" He asked.

"Come and see, Lord," they replied.

Jesus wept.

Then the Jews said, "See how He loved him!"

But some of them said, "Could not He who opened the eyes of the blind man have kept this man from dying?"

Jesus, once more deeply moved, came to the tomb. It was a cave with a stone laid across the entrance. "Take away the stone," He said.

"But, Lord," said Martha, the sister of the dead man, "by this time there is a bad odor, for he has been there four days."

Then Jesus said, "Did I not tell you that if you believed, you would see the glory of God?"

So they took away the stone. Then Jesus looked up and said, "Father, I thank You that You have heard Me. I knew that You always hear Me, but I said this for the benefit of the people standing here, that they may believe that You sent Me."

When He had said this, Jesus called in a loud voice, "Lazarus, come out!" The dead man came out, his hands and feet wrapped with strips of linen, and a cloth around his face.

Jesus said to them, "Take off the grave clothes and let him go."

Recently, two medical researchers ran a fascinating experiment using a dead body. Operating skillfully, they removed the brain from the cadaver and connected the nerve endings to electrical impulses. By pushing buttons, they could send signals to the nerves in the body, which controlled the muscles. They could make the body sit up, move its arms, legs, fingers, blink its eyes, even inhale and exhale. They could even force the heart to beat.

But the body was still a dead body.

There is one question which churns in the gut of all humankind. It is a wrenching, fearsome question which causes even the bravest to shudder. It was first asked by Job, but is still asked by every one of us: "If a man dies, will he live again?" (Job 14:14).

On a sunny afternoon in April, in the little village of Bethany just outside the walls of Jerusalem, Jesus answered humankind's question with a resounding "YES!"

Not only did He answer it in word, when He said to Mary, "Your brother will rise again," but He answered it with the most awesome demonstration of God's power ever witnessed on earth. He spoke life back into the body of an adult man who had been dead and buried four days.

The story begins when the two sisters, deeply concerned that their brother Lazarus was dying, sent desperate word to Jesus who was almost a day's journey away—begging Him to come. They knew He had the power to heal the sick. They knew if He would come, Lazarus would be well again.

Now a man named Lazarus was sick. He was from Bethany, the village of Mary and her sister Martha. This Mary, whose brother Lazarus now lay sick, was the same one who poured perfume on the Lord and wiped His feet with her hair. So the sisters sent word to Jesus, "Lord, the one You love is sick." (John 11:1-3)

Mary, Martha, and their brother Lazarus lived in the little community of Bethany, a suburb of Jerusalem just two miles outside the old wall of the city. The village, almost at the foot of the Mount of Olives, was hidden among groves of olive, fig, and almond trees. It was at the very edge of the desert hills. In fact, the top of the Mount of Olives was the dividing line. The Bethany side of the mountain was green and lush, the western side dry and barren as the desert began and stretched without sign of human habitation all the way to the Dead Sea.

Today, with the growth of Jerusalem, Bethany is actually a part of the metropolitan area.

These three—Mary, Martha, and Lazarus, living together as Mideastern people still do—were very close friends of Jesus. On His visits to Jerusalem, He stayed in their home. He was comfortable in their presence. They did things together as young people would.

For several weeks Jesus had been on the eastern side of the Jordan River in the region of Peraea, probably in the little village of Bethabara. Most of His time there had been spent teaching, using parables as His primary method. It was probably at Bethabara where He told that wonderful story of the Prodigal Son.

Jesus was becoming more and more explicit about His mission. He was beginning to tell people who He actually was. During Hanukkah, three months earlier, He had been in Jerusalem. A large number of people had followed Him around, and one of them asked in a public meeting, "If

You are the Christ, tell us plainly" (John 10:24).

"I did tell you, but you did not believe," Jesus answered. As soon as He said it, they picked up stones and tried to kill Him. "Even though you do not believe Me, believe the miracles," Jesus shouted as they threw their stones. "You must understand that the Father is in Me, and I in the Father" (John 10:38).

Screaming that He was a blasphemer, they rushed Him—attempting to kill Him. As Jesus had been forced to do in Nazareth at the beginning of His ministry, He once again walked through the crowd unharmed and fled through the Judean hills to the place along the Jordan River where John had baptized many people. Here, just beyond Jericho, He forded the river (even though it was at flood stage) and went to the village of Bethabara where He taught, safe from the blood-thirsty mobs in Jerusalem.

He was in Bethabara when word came from Mary and Martha that Lazarus was dying.

> When He heard this, Jesus said, "This sickness will not end in death. No, it is for God's glory so that God's Son may be glorified through it." Jesus loved Martha and her sister and Lazarus. Yet when He heard that Lazarus was sick, He stayed where He was two more days.
>
> Then He said to His disciples, "Let us go back to Judea."
>
> "But Rabbi," they said, "a short while ago the Jews tried to stone You, and yet You are going back there?"
>
> Jesus answered, "Are there not twelve hours of daylight? A man who walks by day will not stumble, for he sees by this world's light. It is when he walks by night that he stumbles, for he has no light."
>
> After He had said this, He went on to tell them, "Our friend Lazarus has fallen asleep, but I am going

there to wake him up."

His disciples replied, "Lord, if he sleeps, he will get better." Jesus had been speaking of his death, but His disciples thought He meant natural sleep.

So then He told them plainly, "Lazarus is dead, and for your sake I am glad I was not there, so that you may believe. But let us go to him."

Then Thomas (called Didymus) said to the rest of the disciples, "Let us also go, that we may die with him."

On His arrival, Jesus found that Lazarus had already been in the tomb for four days. Bethany was less than two miles from Jerusalem, and many Jews had come to Martha and Mary to comfort them in the loss of their brother. When Martha heard that Jesus was coming, she went out to meet Him, but Mary stayed at home.

(John 11:4-20)

One of the factors used by literary critics to prove or disprove authorship is a study of characters. If it can be proved the characters in a novel act inconsistently, that is, a man with a hot temper in chapter one is exposed to an angry situation in chapter four but does not explode, it may prove there were several people writing the book— or that the author lacked the ability to truly relate facts.

There is no such problem in the Bible. Luke, writing many years before John, told a little story about a visit Jesus made to the home of Mary and Martha. In fact, it is the first time we are introduced to these "odd couple" sisters, so different in behavior and character, yet so dedicated to Jesus. Luke tells of a practical Martha, who stayed in the kitchen doing the cooking and preparing the meal. Mary was the pensive sister, sentimental, highly emotional. While her sister was busy with the practical things, Mary was sitting at the feet of Jesus.

In another story Jesus was visiting in the house of the two sisters. Martha, as usual, was serving. Mary, however, overcome by her love for Jesus, reacted true to her spontaneous character. "Then Mary took about a pint of pure nard, an expensive perfume; she poured it on Jesus' feet and wiped His feet with her hair" (John 12:3).

Now we find the two sisters continuing true to character as John tells the story of their reactions to the death of their brother and Jesus' late arrival. Martha, the outspoken activist, rushed out to meet Jesus, chiding Him for arriving too late. Mary remained in the house, heart-broken, weeping. If a literary critic were to examine these characterizations which appear in Luke and John he would have to say, "These stories were not written by two men. They have the same author." Indeed they do. One author (the Holy Spirit), but two penmen—Luke and John.

> "Lord," Martha said to Jesus, "if You had been here, my brother would not have died."

Typical of Martha, she remonstrated with Jesus, reprimanding him with a curt: "Why weren't You here when we needed You?"

I can hear my mother now. She thinks I'm lost. She thinks I've been run over by a truck. She doesn't know where I am. She's deeply concerned. She's been calling all over town trying to find me. She's been praying for me. Then I walk in the house. I've been out playing and I've forgotten the time. I'm perfectly all right. But instead of rushing to gather me in her arms, she begins to scream, rebuking me. "You've worried me to death. You've made me miserable. I've almost had a nervous breakdown worrying about you. Don't you ever do that again. . . ." Then, after the storm of her own anxiety has passed, she finally hugs me and says she's grateful I'm safe.

Such is the nature of grief. It always contains an element of anger and blame. "If You had . . ." Martha screamed at Jesus. How typical to blame God when things go wrong. But we all do it.

> *"But I know that even now God will give You whatever You ask."*

It's an interesting thing about human nature. Nearly all reactions to human events are negative in the beginning. Whatever happens, there is usually an initial negative reaction—followed by a positive reaction. It's easily seen in personal counseling situations. A wife will come in and talk about how terrible her husband is. But after an hour of unloading—venting her anger and frustration—she'll often sit back and say, "but I don't want you to think he's all bad."

This is the approach used by Martha. After fussing with Jesus, she calms down and says, "Still, I know You are who You are, and whatever You want, You can get done." It is an honest, not a manipulative statement. She really believed—as far as her knowledge would allow.

> *Jesus said to her, "Your brother will rise again."*
> *Martha answered, "I know he will rise again in the resurrection at the last day."*

This is a remarkable statement in itself, since there was virtually no understanding of a resurrection at that time. There were two basic schools of thought among the Jews, reflected by the two major religious parties.

The Sadducees were a priestly party who came to prominence after the time of the Maccabees, about 150 years before the birth of Jesus. They were both religious and political. Aristocratic, many of them had wealth, which forced them into a policy of co-operating with the Romans. Unlike the Pharisees, who believed not only in the five books of Moses but also in the huge amount of Oral law, called the Talmud, the Sadducees limited their beliefs to the written word. They denied any doctrine of future resurrection of the body, which they said could not be found in the law.

On the other hand, the Pharisees, who were scribes, (students of the law of Moses and the Oral law of the ancient rabbis), had a fuzzy concept of some kind of resurrection. It was an undefined belief that there was life after death. They didn't know much about it, nor did they know how it happened. They tied it in with the teaching of the law. They thought by keeping the law they would rise from the dead. They related it back to that marvelous word that came out of Job: "I know that my Redeemer lives, and that in the end He will stand upon the earth. And after my skin has been destroyed, yet in my flesh I will see God; I myself will see Him with my own eyes—I, and not another" (Job 19:25-27).

The best the Jews could come up with, with their limited revelation, was the concept of a shadowy place after death called "Sheol." Sheol was neither heaven nor hell, but an abode of the dead. When you died, you didn't disappear, you went to Sheol.

Most cultures of that day had some kind of concept of life after death. The Romans and Greeks, who borrowed and adapted from each other, had a rather ill-defined concept of life after death—but it was all misery. When you died, you were picked up by a spirit, carried to a place call the River Styx, then ferried across the river to a shadowy state of existence.

Although the Greek and Roman legends of life after death were birthed in the human heart—a heart created by God to believe in the afterlife—the Jewish concept was based on godly (but limited) revelation.

When Jesus—the full revelation of God—arrived, He brought with Him a clearly defined teaching on both heaven and hell. Hell was the afterlife apart from God, a determination made on this side of the grave. Heaven was life after death in the presence of God, determined by a man's relationship with God's Son prior to dying.

One of the clearest growths in the Bible is the growth of this belief in life after death. It can be traced through the Old Testament from Job's earliest statement to David's statements concerning Sheol: "If I make my bed in sheol, You are there" (Psalm 139:8), and his hope of heaven: "You guide me with Your counsel, and afterward You will take me into glory. Whom have I in heaven but You: And being with You, I desire nothing on earth" (Psalm 73:23-25).

As one ancient writer said: "The enigmas of life become at least less baffling when we come to rest in the thought that this is not the last act of the human drama." Therefore, when Martha answered Jesus, she bore witness to the highest reach of her faith—"I know that he will rise again in the resurrection at the last day."

Jesus, however, had something far greater in mind—which was obviously the reason He waited several days following His friends' message that Lazarus was dying before coming to Bethany. (Indeed, by the time Jesus received the message, Lazarus was already dead—which Jesus knew by revelation.) They had all seen His healing miracles. In fact, there had been at least two other incidents when Jesus had raised people from the dead. Matthew, Mark, and Luke all record the story of the raising of Jairus' daughter (Matthew 9:18-26; Mark 5:22-43; Luke 8:41-56). Luke also told the story of the raising of the widow's son at Nain (Luke 7:11-17). But in both cases, the children were raised immediately after they died, giving rise to a skepticism that the children might have been in comas. But to raise a man who had been dead four days, a man whose body had been wrapped in grave clothes and sealed in a grave . . . that was another matter.

Jesus had something He wanted His disciples to know—something which would be extremely important on the following Friday when He, Himself, would be put to death. It was as though He were saying, "No, no, life begins here in a relationship with God, and continues on. The physical act of death does not interrupt in any way what is going on in the spirit." The spirit continues to live on. It doesn't even go through a transition. Real life, that which exists in the spirit rather than the body, lives forever, and if you are one of those "in Christ," you move right on into the presence of God. That thing all men cry for and desire—a closer walk with God—is accomplished, has its final fulfillment in the act of death and the instant subsequent act called the "resurrection."

> *Jesus said to her, "I am the resurrection and the life. He who believes in Me will live, even though he dies; and whoever lives and believes in Me will never die. Do you believe this?"*

The question most of us ask is not do I believe it, but do I understand it? I can believe it a lot easier than I can understand it. What does it mean: "I am the resurrection and the life, he who believes in Me will live even though he dies; he who lives and believes in Me will never die"?

Martha is unable to answer Jesus' question. But she is able to answer the unasked question which was even greater than the one He asked.

"I believe, Lord, that You are the Christ, the Son of God who was to come into the world," Martha said. "You are the Messiah. I believe that You are the Messiah."

Martha's answer was the right one. It's not a matter of *what* I believe, it's *who* I believe. "I believe You are the Christ, the Son of God."

Once we understand what Jesus was asking her, and once we understand her answer, we can understand what He is saying to her. He says, "Do you believe that I am the anointed Son standing here in the flesh, not only a godly man, but God Himself?" The early fathers described Him as "very God." If we understand that, that God was standing in front of Martha looking like an ordinary man, then we can understand what He means when He says, "If you have linked your life to Me, if you have related your life to Me, if you have allowed the Spirit that is in Me to come into you, your life will continue on—you will live on as I live on. If you don't believe that, you are separated from Me."

Martha could not comprehend that, of course, for she did not know that Jesus, Himself, was going to be killed just one week from that time and three days later rise from the dead. But in a tremendous burst of faith she grasped something in her spirit that her mind had no way of understanding.

> *"Yes, Lord," she told Him, "I believe that You are the Christ, the Son of God, who was to come into the world."*

This spiritual understanding—that Jesus was the Messiah—is the same kind of revelation received by Peter at Caesarea Philippi and by several others Jesus had healed. Immediately upon receiving it, she felt compelled to tell her sister. It was the same kind of compelling that Andrew felt three years before when he came to his own understanding, following the baptism of Jesus in the Jordan River, that Jesus was God. Rushing to his brother Simon (later called Peter), he cried out, "We have found the Messiah" (John 1:41).

> *After she had said this, she went back and called her sister Mary aside. "The Teacher is here," she said, "and is asking for you." When Mary heard this, she got up quickly and went to Him. Now Jesus had not yet entered the village, but was still at the place where Martha had met Him. When the Jews who had been with Mary in the house, comforting her, noticed how quickly she got up and went out, they followed her, supposing she was going to the tomb to mourn there.*

A large crowd of mourners had gathered around the tomb of Lazarus. In many cases those who came to weep were professional mourners, people who attended funerals and for a small fee wept appropriately. Such was not the case with Lazarus, however. His family, his friends, were genuinely moved. Their tears were real. They were weeping profusely, with unrestrained wailing and shrieking, for it was the Jewish custom that the more unrestrained the weeping, the more honor was paid the dead. (It was for this reason professional mourners were often hired to give even more honor.)

> *When Jesus saw her [Mary] weeping, and the Jews who had come along with her also weeping, He was deeply moved in spirit and troubled. "Where have you laid him?" He asked.*
> *"Come and see, Lord," they replied.*
> *Jesus wept.*
> *Then the Jews said, "See how He loved him!"*

So deeply did Jesus enter into the wounded hearts and sorrows of His friends that His heart was wrenched with anguish. Even though He knew what was about to take place, He wept with His friends. Had the Jews been in tune with the spirit of Jesus, they would not have said, "See how He loved him!" Rather, they would have said, "See how He loves them!"

It is necessary, in this case, to remember to whom this Gospel was written. John, the writer, had been exiled on the Greek isle of Patmos to live out his last days. It was there he had a great revelation from God, perhaps while writing his biography of Jesus, which he also wrote down. That writing became known as the book of Revelation. This biography, however, unlike the biography written by Matthew, was written for Gentiles—and, in particular, the Greeks. To the Greek, the primary characteristic of God was what they called *apatheia*. This goes beyond our English word *apathy* to mean the total inability to feel any emotion whatsoever. Any show of emotion was looked upon as weakness.

The argument was this: If you feel joy or sorrow, happiness or grief, you are under the control of another person or another situation. That means you are not strong, that another has power over you. The moment that happens, that person is greater than you. Therefore, since no one is more powerful than God, it is impossible for God to feel emotion.

What a wonderful picture Jesus gave us of God. God is not lonely, isolated, passionless. God feels our sorrows, our misery, our anxiety. He weeps with us. He also feels our elation, our joy, our relief—and He laughs with us. The greatest thing Jesus taught us about God is that He is a God who cares.

There are many examples of this. In the late 1940s, Oral Roberts took his tent ministry across middle America to the poor whites and even poorer blacks. He had only one message. God is a good God. It was a foreign message, for the churches of the day, by and large, had pictured God as a god of the middle class and the rich, a god helpless before sickness and poverty, a god who gave blessings to a favored few but let the rest of the people suffer. Roberts, with his tent meetings, invited in the poor, the sick, the homeless, and told them God was good. People came, believed, and were healed.

Later, in the 1960s, another Pentecostal preacher, David Wilkerson, went into the ghettos of New York and told the gang leaders, the youthful warlords of the streets, "God is love." Nicky Cruz, one of the most vicious of those young gang leaders, snarled at Wilkerson. Drawing his switch-blade, he told him he was going to cut him to pieces. "Go ahead," the preacher replied, "but if you cut me into a thousands pieces, each piece will cry out, 'God loves you.'" The message of this good God was too much for Cruz. He gave his heart to Christ and became one of the world's foremost evangelists.

God cares!

If anything touches the heart of God, it is our inability to understand who He is. We continue in our own struggles of life without giving Him the glory and the credit, or even allowing Him to be the kind of God He wants to be. He wants to be a God of miracles. He wants to be a God of resurrection. He wants to be a God of power and provision in our lives. But because we can't get our eyes up, because our eyes are always horizontal rather than vertical, we miss the countless miracles which are waiting for those who believe—who give Him glory.

To understand the extent of this miracle we need to understand what took place in the burial. There was a time in Israel when a burial was exceedingly costly. The body was anointed with the finest spices and ointments for the sake of preservation and to keep down the stench of invariable decay. The body was then dressed in an incredibly expensive robe. All kinds of valuable treasures and possessions were buried in the tomb along with the body. It became a mark of social status as to how elaborate the funeral was—thus, the paying of the mourners. In fact, proper burial had become an almost intolerable burden for poor people.

It was up to a rabbi named Gamaliel the Second to change this. He gave orders that when he died, he was to be buried in a simple linen robe. Today, at funerals, Jews often drink a cup to Rabbi Gamaliel who rescued them from extravagance. Since the time of Gamaliel, the dead body has been wrapped in grave bandages, each limb wrapped separately, and dressed in a simple linen shroud sometimes called by the beautiful name of "the traveling dress."

Funerals were as ceremonial as the weddings in Jesus' day. In the procession to the tomb, the women mourners went first, based on the ancient Jewish belief that it was woman who by her first sin brought death into the world. After memorial speeches were made at the tomb, the people withdrew to the family house where the mourning continued for seven days. During this time all the furniture was turned against the wall and mourners sat on the ground or low stools.

The grave was either a pile of stones or a cave. In the case of Lazarus, it was a natural cave cut into deep rock. The body was actually placed in a site hewn out of the cave, winding down several levels to perhaps 30 feet below the surface. Once the body was prepared and placed in the cave, a rock was rolled over the opening, sealing it to keep out the wild animals and flesh-eating birds of prey.

> *Jesus, once more deeply moved, came to the tomb. It was a cave with a stone laid across the entrance. "Take away the stone," He said.*
>
> *"But, Lord," said Martha, the sister of the dead man, "by this time there is a bad odor, for he has been there four days."*
>
> *Then Jesus said, "Did I not tell you that if you believed, you would see the glory of God?"*

Practical Martha could think of only one thing: the grim, repulsive, putrifying corpse of her brother. Jews believed that the spirit of the departed one hovered around the tomb for four days, seeking some way to re-enter the body. At the end of four days, however, when the body was so decayed it was no longer recognizable, the spirit left for Sheol. Understanding this gives even deeper meaning to the words of Jesus to the criminal who was dying beside Him on the cross: "I tell you the truth, today you will be with Me in paradise" (Luke 23:43).

How true it is. No one wants his decaying parts exposed. To have the full light of Jesus shine into our lives would reveal many dead areas. We don't want to be exposed. We don't want the stone rolled away. If the stone is rolled away, if anybody takes a look inside of us, there will be a big stink. If we only knew that the light of Jesus never causes a stink, it only produces resurrection.

> *So they took away the stone. Then Jesus looked up and said, "Father, I thank You that You have heard Me. I knew that You always hear Me, but I said this for the benefit of the people standing here, that they may believe that You sent Me."*

It is an interesting and revealing prayer. "Lord, what

I'm doing is for Your glory, not to draw attention to Myself.
I want these people to know who You really are, and that's
the only reason for this miracle which is about to take
place."

> When He had said this, Jesus called in a loud voice,
> "Lazarus, come out!" The dead man came out, his hands
> and feet wrapped with strips of linen, and a cloth around
> his face.

Far below, in the dark tomb, the grinding noise from
above disturbed the bats as the rock was rolled back. Then,
ringing down the winding passage, came the authoritative
shout that ever since has echoed into the hearts of all
hopeless men and women: "LAZARUS, COME FORTH!"

With a word, all the processes of death were reversed.
Time was turned around. There was a great stirring as
Life returned to the body—Life which was given at the
mere word of God. Thousands of years before, walking
with His Father through the Garden of Eden, Jesus had
watched God pick up dirt, mold it into the form of a man,
then, breathing into the nostrils of that dead form, declare,
"Hayyim"—Life.

That was what Jesus did when He shouted down the
tomb. "Hayyim"—Life. And Lazarus, stumbling in his grave
clothes, crawled out into the hot afternoon sun.

> Jesus said to them, "Take off the grave clothes and
> let him go."

It is not enough to have life. We need to be free. So
many of us have experienced life but have never tasted
the freedom of the Holy Spirit. We're still bound in our
grave clothes. We need to ask ourselves the question: Am
I alive or dead? If I am alive, am I still bound in the

old grave wrappings of sin and tradition? Do I need someone to help me, or do I prefer to remain in the shadows?

Jesus sought only the glory of God. When Elijah had his encounter with the prophets of Baal on Mount Carmel he prayed, "Answer me, O Lord, answer me so these people will know that You, O Lord, are God. . . ." (1 Kings 18:37). Jesus never did anything to draw attention to Himself. His single purpose on earth was to glorify His Father in heaven. How different men are, even men of God, who seem to do everything to draw attention to themselves. So much of what we do is an attempt, by our own power, to raise ourselves in the eyes of others. What we wear, how (and where) we live, our transportation, our jewelry, our cosmetics—all frequently are designed to bring glory to self. It was by God, and for God, that Jesus acted. It may be that there would be more miracles in our lives if we, too, ceased to act by our own strength and for our own self and began acting only in the power of God and for His glory.

One day I decided I wanted to find out what the world looked like as a small child. I got down on the floor with my three-year-old grandson and walked around on my knees. Everything was different from that perspective. I thought, what would it be like if I had to walk through life less than three feet tall? I would never be able to see facial expressions. I would be acquainted with knees rather than noses. It would be almost impossible to understand the world of adults.

Perhaps that's what Jesus was weeping about. He so wanted His friends to understand God, but they were earthbound instead. It took a miracle to bring revelation—much as if God had picked us up in His arms and said, "Come up here for a minute and see what the Kingdom is really like. Up here you understand what authority you really have—even authority over death." With a word, time was turned around. It was just a few miles from there, in the valley of Ajalon, that 1,000 years before Joshua had pointed to the sun and the moon and commanded them to stand still. Everything had stopped so that God's people could get their job done. Here Jesus pointed at time and said, "Go back." And Lazarus came forth from the grave.

Several years ago I received a letter from a prisoner on death row at the Florida State Penitentiary in Starke, Florida. A dozen years before, Carl Songer, just 20 years of age, had walked away from a prison work release program in Oklahoma where he was finishing his sentence for stealing an automobile. Joy-riding through Florida at Christmas with a friend, they parked in an orange grove to spend the night. They were awakened early in the morning by an inquiring state trooper. Both boys panicked. Carl had a gun hidden under the seat. When the trooper looked into the car at the frightened boys, Carl shot and killed him. A jury sentenced him to die in Florida's electric chair.

After years of languishing in a lonely cell on death row as the endless appeals went on, Carl was given a Bible. It came from another death row prisoner, Carl Spekelink, the night before Spekelink was executed. While in prison, Spekelink had accepted Jesus Christ. He wanted young Carl Songer to have his Bible.

Songer put the Bible on a shelf in his cell. He was not interested in religion. He had seen the religious programs on TV. He had heard the various television preachers crying out in favor of the death penalty. It was hard to listen to someone who wants to kill you. Songer was searching for life, not death.

Night after night in his lonely cell, Carl Songer sat on the edge of his cot trying to figure out what life was all about. He was searching, he told me later, for purpose. Then one evening, an evening like all other evenings, he was aware of another "presence" in the cell with him. He described it as a light somewhere over his head. But when he raised his head to look up, the light moved back. He never could see it, but nevertheless it was clear and distinct—just out of reach.

Frightened, he said, "God, is that You?"

Instantly the light, in a mighty WHOOOSH, came over his head and into his chest. Instead of the light being above him, it was now radiating out of him. He began to cry.

The crying continued for several days. During that time Carl said he saw himself from an entirely different perspective. For the first time he realized he was not just an innocent kid, as his defense lawyers had tried to convince the jury. He was a murderer. He had taken a man's life. He had taken the son of loving parents, the husband of a young wife, the father of a little boy. He was a cold-blooded murderer and he deserved his punishment.

This revelation of self was followed by two days of anguished repentance. During this time, he took the Bible off the shelf and opened it to Matthew. Even though he could not understand the genealogies, he was convinced that it was God who had come into him and since this was God's book, he needed to read it.

The following night he turned to the Gospel of John. There he read: "In the beginning was the Word, and the Word was with God, and the Word was God. . . . The Word became flesh and lived for a while among us. . . ." (John 1:1, 14). Suddenly, he realized Jesus was God. It was Jesus who had come into his heart. The tears returned, but this time they were tears of joy. For the first time in his young life, he had purpose.

Sometime after that he read one of my books and wrote me. His execution date had been set. Twice before, the governor had signed death warrants, but his lawyers had gotten stays of execution. This was his third time to the death house, and even his attorneys said they had exhausted all hope. Carl wanted me to come up and spend the last night with him in his cell on death watch, then be present to witness his execution at 7:00 a.m. the next morning.

I agreed. I knew I could not go just for the execution, but needed to meet this remarkable young man before that fateful evening. I made a number of trips back and forth to the state penitentiary to visit him. I was deeply impressed with his gentle faith, his love for God, his repentant spirit, his forgiving attitude toward those who had put him in prison and were going to execute him.

On the eve of his execution, I was leaving my nearby motel to spend the night with Carl in his cell next to the electric chair. We had planned to stay up reading the Bible and singing songs of praise. Carl was looking forward to meeting God the next morning and wanted to use the night as a time of great celebration—a jubilant "going away" party, so to speak.

But, as I was leaving the motel, a reporter from one of the national TV networks who was in town covering the execution ran up to me. "Word has just come over our wire service," the reporter said. "The U.S. Supreme Court has agreed that Carl Songer did not receive a fair sentence. His execution has been delayed indefinitely while the review courts examine whether he should have been sentenced to death or merely given a long-term prison sentence."

I was the one who walked into Carl's cell and broke the news. He was not going to heaven the next morning after all. That would have to wait. God had an additional purpose for him on earth.

"How do you feel?" I asked.

"Like Lazarus," he grinned, shaking his head. "I praise God for the news, but in my mind I was already in heaven. I'm not sure I like being called back."

As I write this, Carl is still in prison. But he has been used by God, as Carl Spekelink was used, to pass along Bibles and other forms of good news to a number of his friends who are facing death without hope. Perhaps that's the highest purpose to which one can be called.

What became of Lazarus after his resurrection? There is no record, but the ancient legends say he always seemed to be a bit melancholy—as if he had experienced something wonderful that no one else could fully understand. For as wonderful as it is to be called back from the dead, it is far more wonderful to receive resurrection into life eternal.

Father, I believe it is possible. I stand with You. Not only do You give life; You are alive. I thank You for giving us the power and authority to say, as Jesus said, "Come forth." For His sake, and for Your glory. Amen.

Where Eagles Soar

by Jamie Buckingham

"Watch the eagle," our guide said, pointing high above the desert at the silent figure soaring close to the mountains. "He locks his wings, picks the thermals and rides the breath of God above the storm."

What do Christians need to take them over the storms that confront them? The Bible is not enough. In fact, without the Spirit to interpret it, we may even be led astray. We need the Spirit—the breath of God—to make the written word come alive.

But that is not all. The Spirit wants to do more than speak to us—he wants to take over our lives.

This book challenges us to venture out like the eagle and enter a life beyond our own control.

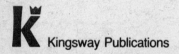

Kingsway Publications

The Hot Line

by Peter H. Lawrence

'This is the beginner's book written by a beginner for beginners,' says Peter Lawrence. 'It is a veritable collection of signs and blunders, with laughter one minute and tears the next...God loves some decidedly odd people. This book is written by one of them.'

Many Christians today are willing to accept that God does speak to people. However, it is often difficult to discern the voice of God.

From his own experience over the past fifteen years Peter Lawrence offers guidance on the costly but enthralling path of obedience to God. 'Learning to recognise, receive, test and give "words" from God is just like learning any other discipline. There are no easy answers and there is no cheap grace.'

'Superbly written. It is humerous, self-deprecating, profoundly honest (especially about failure) and intensely readable...Remember that the same God is your God and can do as much through you.'

Michael Green

THE REV PETER LAWRENCE has been Vicar of Christ Church, Burney Lane, Birmingham since 1979. He and his wife Carol have three daughters. He is a keen sportsman and former English teacher.

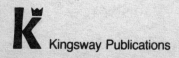

Kingsway Publications